Storybook Parties

45 Parties Based on Children's Favorite Stories

Penny Warner & Liya Lev Oertel

Meadowbrook Press

Distributed by Simon & Schuster
New York

Library of Congress Cataloging-in-Publication Data
Warner, Penny.
     Storybook parties: 45 parties based on children's favorite stories / Penny
Warner & Liya Lev Oertel
         p.   cm.
     ISBN 0-88166-389-1 (Meadowbrook) ISBN 0-689-84328-3 (Simon & Schuster)
     1. Children's parties. 2. Children's stories. I. Title: 45 parties based on chil-
dren's favorite stories. II. Title: Forty-five parties based on children's favorite
stories. III. Oertel, Liya Lev. IV. Title.

GV1205 .W3794 2001
793.2'1—dc21
                                              00-048194

Managing Editor: Christine Zuchora-Walske
Copyeditors: Kathleen Martin-James, Angela Wiechmann
Proofreader: Megan McGinnis
Production Manager: Paul Woods
Desktop Publishing: Danielle White
Illustrations: Darcy Bell-Myers
Index: Beverlee Day

© 2001 by Liya Lev Oertel and Penny Warner

Published by Meadowbrook Press, 5451 Smetana Drive, Minnetonka, MN 55343

www.meadowbrookpress.com

BOOK TRADE DISTRIBUTION by Simon & Schuster, a division of Simon and
Schuster, Inc., 1230 Avenue of the Americas, New York, NY 10020

05 04 03 02 01   10 9 8 7 6 5 4 3 2 1

Printed in the United States of America

Dedication

To our storybook families . . .
Penny's: Tom, Matt, and Rebecca
Liya's: Jens and Jacob

Acknowledgments

We thank each other for simplifying the process and improving the final product. Thanks also to Christine Zuchora-Walske, Megan McGinnis, Angie Wiechmann, and Kathleen Martin-James for their great editing skills and to Bruce Lansky, our publisher, who makes dreams come true.

Contents

Parties for Nine- to Twelve-Year-Olds

Introduction

Children love stories of all kinds. They love imagining themselves in the stories, having adventures like Tom Sawyer or snooping around like Harriet the Spy. They love the thrills of *Robin Hood*, the chills of *Bunnicula,* and the magic of *Harry Potter.* In *Storybook Parties,* you will find easy ways to bring children's favorite stories to life.

The parties are divided into three sections: *Parties for Three- to Six-Year-Olds, Parties for Six- to Nine-Year-Olds,* and *Parties for Nine- to Twelve-Year-Olds.* We have grouped the stories by the age children generally are when they first read them. The beauty of a good story, however, is that it is ageless. If your twelve-year-olds are crazy about Winnie-the-Pooh, throw them a Pooh party. Don't feel restricted by our categories.

To prepare for your storybook party, read the book with your child. Read it several times, if you like, and talk about the characters, the plot, and what makes the book so special. Then ask the invited guests to read the story, too, so they'll be prepared for the related fun, food, games, and activities. If everyone is familiar with the book, the party will be more meaningful for all who participate.

Your party will take some planning and preparation, so choose a special occasion like a birthday party, a slumber party, a summer get-together, or a playgroup gathering. Or start a book club and bring a different storybook to life each time you meet.

We've chosen forty-five popular children's books and provided a complete party for each story.

Every chapter gives step-by-step instructions for creating invitations, decorations, refreshments, and party favors based on the story theme. With a little imagination, you can make creative invitations that look like treasure maps, puzzles, or "radiant" cobwebs. You can transform a family room into a forest, a playroom into a palace, a schoolroom into a sailing ship, or a back yard into a beach. And you can serve snacks that look like paw prints, upside-down sundaes, or bugs!

The best part about a storybook party is the excitement of seeing your favorite literature come to life. Storybook parties foster children's love for reading and inspire their imaginations and creativity. They increase children's vocabulary, language skills, social interaction, and problem-solving ability. Best of all, they're exciting, adventurous, mysterious, romantic, and just plain fun!

So pick out your children's favorite story and watch their excitement as they take part in a storybook party!

The Cat in the Hat

When the Cat in the Hat magically appears on the doorstep, all kinds of mysterious "things" begin to happen—just ask Thing 1 and Thing 2. Have your own *Cat in the Hat* party and watch the surprises appear with the Cat!

Invitation

Where's the Cat? In the Hat!

1. Fold a sheet of white paper in half.
2. Cut out the Cat in the Hat's hat, making sure the top of the hat is on the fold.
3. Color red and white stripes on the hat.
4. Open the hat and draw or glue a picture of the Cat in the Hat inside.
5. Write "What Fun We Can Have!" inside along with the party details.

Costumes

Ask guests to come dressed as characters from the book or deck them out in *The Cat in the Hat* accessories when they arrive. Give the guests large bow ties made from thick red ribbon. Pin on tails made from ties stuffed with cotton batting or of drapery cord that's frayed at one end. Supply blue wigs so the guests can pretend to be Thing 1 and Thing 2.

Decorations

- Draw raindrops on the window using washable markers. Draw pictures of the children from the book. Tape them to the window as if they are looking out and greeting the guests.

- Write phrases from the book on large sheets of white paper, decorate them with pictures of the characters, and tape them to the walls. Use them as place mats as well.
- Create Thing 1 and Thing 2 dolls from red one-piece infant outfits or tights and long-sleeve tops. Make heads from balls covered with socks. Draw faces on the heads with markers and top them with blue yarn wigs.

- Paint large boxes red and tie them with red ribbon. Fill them with items you'll use at the party.
- Set out items from the book, such as an umbrella, cup, book, toy ship, cake, rake, kite, net, fishbowls with fake or real fish, and so on.

Games

What's in the Box?

Paint some small boxes red. Inside each box put an item that relates to the book, such as a rubber fish, paper umbrella, cup, toy ship, and so on. Blindfold a player. Have her feel the item inside a box and guess what it is. If she guesses correctly, she gets a prize. If not, she keeps the booby prize inside the box. Let each player have a turn feeling inside a box.

What Happens Next?

Read *The Cat in the Hat* out loud to the players. Read the story a second time, but after each page, ask a player to guess what happens next. If he guesses correctly, give him a prize. Make sure everyone has a turn and everyone gets a prize.

Thing Catchers

Divide the players into pairs and ask them to line up opposite their partners. Give one player of each pair a butterfly net and the other a red or white ball. The players with the balls toss them to their partners. The partners have to catch the balls using the nets. After each toss, have the players take a step back to make the game more challenging. If a player misses a

catch, that pair drops out of the game. When only one pair remains, award a prize to them. Have the players switch roles and play again.

Activities

Cat in the Hat Hats

Measure the circumference of each guest's head. Cut a rectangle of white paper as wide as each measurement. Have each kid glue red ribbon on her paper to make horizontal stripes. Glue the paper into cylinders. Have the kids wear their hats and pretend to be the Cat in the Hat.

Go Fly a Kite

Buy some plain kites or make your own out of paper, tongue depressors, and long string. Have the kids decorate the kites with stickers, markers, paint, glitter, and so on. If the day is windy, take the kites outside (when they're dry) and fly them.

Thing 1 and Thing 2

Give the kids red and blue play dough or clay and ask them to make Thing 1 and Thing 2. To make the Things' hair, squeeze blue play dough through a garlic press. If you're using homemade dough, bake the figures at 300°F for an hour or until firm. Let the kids take home their Things.

Favors and Prizes
- *The Cat in the Hat* by Dr. Seuss
- Magic tricks and wands
- Real (check with parents) or fake goldfish in bowls
- Big red and white balls

Tumble Tower

Collect stackable items like books, plastic plates, boxes, blocks, and so on. Make sure you have at least as many items as players. Have the players sit in a circle. The first player chooses an item and sets it in the middle of the circle. The next player sets another item on top of the first item. Each player tries to add to the tower without making it tumble. Play continues until the tower falls. Play again, starting with a different first player.

Refreshments

- Cat in the Hat Cake: Frost a sheet cake blue with red details. Photocopy and color pictures from the book. Glue the pictures to cardboard, leaving extra space at the bottom. Insert the bottoms of the pictures in the cake.
- Milk in saucers (depending upon the age of your guests and your tolerance for spills!) or in regular glasses
- Tuna sandwiches cut into hat shapes
- Fish-shaped crackers in little cups or cat food bowls

Cinderella

If you want to go to the ball, you'll have to ask your Fairy Godmother. Or you could host your own ball with a little help from your mouse friends. All you need are beautiful glass slippers, a lovely gown . . . and maybe a magic wand.

Invitation

Glass Slipper

1. Cut a slipper from a transparent sheet of plastic or plastic-coated fabric.
2. Write the party details on the slipper with a permanent marker.
3. Spread clear glue on the other side of the slipper and sprinkle on silver glitter to make it sparkle. (You can also use glitter glue.)
4. Mail with a little glitter inside the envelope.

Costumes

- Have the guests come dressed in ragged old clothes like those Cinderella wore to do chores. Or ask the guests to come dressed as mice—add noses and whiskers with an eyebrow pencil when they arrive. You or another adult might dress like the Fairy Godmother with a magic wand and a long skirt and shawl.

Decorations

- Create an elegant ballroom with balloons, twinkling lights, and streamers.
- Cut stars from gold or silver poster board, decorate them with glitter, and tape them to chopsticks so they look like magic wands. Attach ribbons near the stars and hang them from the ceiling.
- Play classical music.

- Paint a pumpkin on one side of a large box. On the other side, paint a silver coach. Cut a door on the coach side so the kids can go inside.
- Cut a giant circle from white poster board and paint it to look like a clock. Tack black construction paper hands to the middle of the clock. Move the hands closer and closer to "midnight" as the party progresses. When it's midnight, ring a bell twelve times.

Games

Slipper Shuffle

Pile all the players' shoes in the middle of the room. Have the players stand in a circle around the pile, their backs to the shoes. At the word "Go!" have the players turn around, find their shoes, and put them on. The first player to put on both shoes wins a prize.

Mystery Makeup

Divide the players into pairs. Give each pair bright lipstick and nail polish. In

each pair, have one player be Cinderella and the other be the Fairy Godmother. Blindfold the Fairy Godmother. At the word "Go!" have the Fairy Godmother apply the lipstick to Cinderella and then paint all ten of her nails. The pair that finishes the tasks first wins a prize. The results should be pretty funny, so take photos! Have the pairs switch roles and play again.

Activities

Ball Gowns

Provide guests with lots of colorful crepe paper, tape, scissors, ribbon, and other supplies to create ball gowns. Accessorize with costume jewelry, wigs, glitter makeup, and gloves. Have them wear their ball gowns for the remainder of the party.

Prizes & Favors

- *Cinderella* or a collection of fairy tales
- Makeup
- Pumpkins
- Costume jewelry
- Magic wands

Slipper Fashion

Provide the kids with pink or white socks. Let the guests create their own fancy slippers with decorating supplies, such as fabric paints, glitter glue, stick-on jewels, ribbon, permanent markers, and buttons. Have a foot fashion show when the slippers are finished.

Cinderella Hairstyles

Set out hair accessories, such as brushes, combs, hair clips, ribbons, hair spray, temporary hair colors, and mirrors. Let the guests do one another's hair in fancy styles, like the hairstyle Cinderella wore at the ball. For added fun, supply wigs and other hair extensions. For even more fun, hire a hairstylist to give tips and do the guests' hair in wild styles.

Refreshments

- Fancy appetizers on fine china
- Sandwiches on tinted bread (ordered from the bakery)
- Variety of cheeses (for the mice)
- Sparkling apple cider in plastic champagne glasses
- Pumpkin Cake: Frost a round cake orange and add pumpkin details with chocolate and green frosting.

Clifford, the Big Red Dog

Clifford is not just a dog. Clifford is a big red dog. In fact, Clifford is a very big red dog! And big red dogs like to have parties, just as kids do. Host a *Clifford* party and invite your friends to share in the king-size fun!

Invitation

Big Red Dog

1. Fold a large sheet of red construction paper in half.
2. Draw an outline of Clifford on the front and add "Come to Clifford's Big Red Dog Party!"
3. Write the party details inside. Ask the guest to bring a stuffed dog or other stuffed animal to the party.
4. Enclose a small dog biscuit in the large envelope.

Costumes

Suggest that your guests come dressed all in red to match Clifford or ask them to come dressed as dogs or as their favorite animals. You might provide big floppy dog ears made from felt attached to headbands. Then add noses, whiskers, and other dog markings to the guests' faces with face paint.

Decorations

- Construct a doghouse from two large boxes. Cut the top, bottom, and two sides off one box. The remaining two sides will be an inverted V, peaked in the middle, like a roof. Set the inverted V on the other box and secure it with duct tape. Paint the doghouse red and paint Clifford's name on the front in black.

- Create a giant Clifford from red construction paper or from cardboard painted red. Tape it to the wall.
- Hang bone-shaped dog biscuits from the ceiling.
- Place stuffed animals around the room.
- Set out oversize items, such as a giant comb, toothbrush, fork, and so on, to make your guests feel small.
- Make animals out of balloons and place them on the table.
- Make place cards using pictures of different breeds of dogs.

- Play dog-related songs, such as "How Much Is That Doggy in the Window?" or "Hound Dog."

Games

Clifford's Giant Guessing Game

Hide oversize novelty items separately in large paper bags. Let each player feel the item inside each bag and try to guess what it is. Record the kids' guesses on paper. When everyone has guessed, show the items to the

players. Award a prize to the player who guessed the most correct items.

Clifford Can!

Write or draw a task for each player on an index card, such as "Brush your

Prizes and Favors
- *Clifford, the Big Red Dog* by Norman Bridwell
- Stuffed dogs
- Pet supplies, such as collars, nametags, chew toys, food dishes, and so on
- Big red balloons, balls, and so on

teeth," "Braid your hair," "Eat a snack," "Draw a picture," and so on. Ask a player to put on a pair of mittens. Tell him to choose a card and act out the task. The mittens are a reminder that the player can only use his paws! For example, if he chooses "Brush your teeth," he must go through the motions of putting imaginary toothpaste on an imaginary toothbrush, brushing, and rinsing, just like Clifford would. Ask the others to guess what "Clifford" is doing. The first player to correctly guess the task gets a point and the player with the most points wins a prize.

Activities

Dog Biscuits

Using a cookie cutter or knife, cut cookie dough into bone-shaped dog biscuits. Bake the cookies and let the kids decorate them with candy sprinkles and frosting.

Animal Outfits

Set out fabric scraps, crepe paper, glue, and tape. Have the guests make outfits for their stuffed pets. Put on a pet parade when all the outfits are completed. Videotape the parade and show the video during the party.

Dog Dishes

Give each guest a plastic pet dish. Write the names of the guests' stuffed pets on the dishes with a permanent marker. Provide markers, stickers, puffy paints, and other craft items for the kids to use to decorate their dishes.

Refreshments

- Big Red Dog Bone Cake: Set a cupcake at each corner of a loaf cake to make it look like a bone. Frost the bone red.
- Animal crackers, Goldfish crackers, and teddy bear cookies
- Sandwiches cut into animal shapes
- Serve the food in pet dishes.

Curious George

If you're curious like George, a jungle party is the place for you. Come see what the man in the yellow hat has in store!

Invitation

Yellow Hat

1. Cut 2 big hats from yellow construction paper.
2. Glue the top and sides of the hats together but leave the bottom open.
3. Write the party details on one side of the hat.
4. Cut out a picture of Curious George. Make sure he's smaller than the opening at the bottom of the hat.
5. Tape a yellow paper banana to George's hand.
6. Slip George into the hat, leaving his tail sticking out. When the guest pulls the tail, out comes George.
7. Mail the invitation in a large manila envelope and write "George" as the return address.

Costumes

Ask your guests to come dressed all in yellow or as a character in a Curious George book, such as the man in the yellow hat, firefighter, doctor, sailor, or police officer. Or transform the guests into George when they arrive. Give them monkey ears made from stiff brown felt or brown craft foam attached to headbands. Make tails from rope or brown fake fur. Use face paint to make the kids look like monkeys.

Decorations

• Cut large tree trunks from brown construction paper and giant leaves from green construction paper. Tape them to the walls.

- Hang green streamers to create jungle vines.
- Photocopy pictures of George. Float helium balloons to the ceiling and tape the pictures to the balloon strings to make it look as if George is holding onto them.
- Set out bunches of bananas.
- Use bananas as place cards by writing the guests' names on them with permanent marker.

Games

Balloon Catch

Number slips of paper, one for each guest. Wrap as many prizes as there are slips. Roll the slips and insert them into balloons. Fill the balloons with helium. Tie a string to each balloon and attach a cutout of George to the other end of the string. Have the players stand in a circle while you hold onto the balloons. Let go of all the balloons at once and let the players catch balloons before they hit the ceiling.

Players who catch balloons must pop them to find the numbers inside. Match the numbers to the prizes. Winners must sit out while the remaining players catch balloons. Repeat until all the balloons have been caught and each player has a prize.

Favors and Prizes
- *Curious George* or other books in the series by H. A. Rey
- Yellow T-shirts
- Balloon bouquets
- Toy monkeys
- Bunches of bananas and small jars of peanut butter

Where's George?
Buy a Curious George doll or glue a picture of George onto cardboard. Have the players leave the room. Hide George while they're gone. When they return, they must find George. Whoever finds him wins a prize. The winner then drops out of the search but gets to hide George the next time.

Activities

Yellow Hats
Spray-paint straw hats yellow. Give the hats to the kids to decorate with puffy paints, stickers, glitter, ribbon, feathers, and so on.

Monkey Business

Put on some music and have the kids walk like monkeys. Place a rope on the floor and have the kids try to walk on the "jungle vine" without falling into the "quicksand" on either side. Set up an obstacle course and have the kids act like monkeys trying to get from one side of the jungle to the other.

Refreshments

- Banana bread with peanut butter and jelly
- Banana Monkey Shakes: Combine 1 banana with 2 scoops vanilla ice cream and ½ cup milk. Blend the ingredients until smooth. Makes 2 drinks.
- Banana Pops: Cut bananas in half. Insert a tongue depressor into the bottom of each banana half. Spread peanut butter on the bananas and let the kids roll them in coconut, granola, sprinkles, or chopped nuts.

The Gingerbread Man

The Gingerbread Man has been a favorite story for many years. Perhaps kids enjoy the Gingerbread Man's adventure, or maybe they just love gingerbread. Either way, they're sure to love a *Gingerbread Man* party!

Invitation

Gingerbread Kid

1. Using a cookie cutter or a picture as a pattern, cut a gingerbread kid from brown felt and another from brown poster board.
2. Glue the felt figure onto the poster board one.
3. Decorate the front of the figure with puffy paints or markers.
4. Write the party details on the back.
5. Mail in a brown envelope decorated with puffy paints.

Costumes

Ask guests to come dressed all in brown or make gingerbread costumes from brown crepe paper or brown fabric when they arrive. Decorate the gingerbread kids' faces with face paint and give them pink bow ties.

Decorations

- Make an oven out of a big box painted brown. Detail it with black paint or markers. Cut out an oven door.
- Cut gingerbread kids from brown paper or felt. Add details with a marker. Hang them from the ceiling and tape them to the walls.
- Set out pictures or stuffed animals representing the animals the

Gingerbread Man meets on his adventure: a cow, horse, fox, and so on.

- Bake gingerbread kid cookies and label each with a guest's name. Use them as place cards.
- Use a gingerbread house as a centerpiece.

Games

"Can't Catch Me!"

Set the cardboard oven outdoors or on one side of the party room. Choose one player to be the Gingerbread Man and have him crouch behind the oven. Give the rest of the players animal names, such as fox, cow, horse, and so on. Line the animals on either side of the oven, about ten feet away from it. Set a timer for thirty seconds. When the timer goes off, the Gingerbread Man must run across the yard or room while the animals try to catch him. If the Gingerbread Man makes it to the other side without being tagged, he gets a prize. If he gets caught, he trades places with the animal who caught him.

Fix the Gingerbread Kids!

Bake large gingerbread kid cookies. After removing the cookies from the oven, cut them in half using a zigzag pattern, making each pattern slightly different from the others. Separate the cookie halves and give each player a half. Have the players find those who have the other halves of their cookies. The first players to match cookie halves win a prize.

Prizes and Favors
- *The Gingerbread Man*
- Cookie cutters
- Various kinds of cookies

Activities

The Gingerbread Man Play

Using *The Gingerbread Man* as a guide, assign parts to all the guests. Add extra animals if you have more kids than characters. Give each actor a prop, such as an apron for the farmer's wife, a pink bow tie for the Gingerbread Man, horns and a bell for the cow, a tail and ears for the fox, and so on. Read the story to the kids. Then slowly reread the story and have the kids act it out. Videotape the play and show the video during the party.

Gingerbread Houses

Let the guests build gingerbread houses with graham crackers and frosting. Have them dab candies in frosting and stick them to their houses to decorate. Let them choose to either eat their houses or take them home in small boxes.

Refreshments

- Gingerbread cake with cream cheese frosting and small ginger- bread kid cookies on top
- Raisins
- Wheat bread sandwiches cut into gingerbread kid shapes
- Ginger ale

Harold and the Purple Crayon

Whenever Harold has a problem, he draws himself out of it with his purple crayon. If you have a purple crayon and lots of imagination, you can have your own adventures at a *Harold and the Purple Crayon* party!

Invitation

Purple Crayon

1. Fold white construction paper in half.
2. Write "Come to a Harold and the Purple Crayon Party" on the front with a purple crayon.
3. Write the party details inside with a white crayon. The words will be almost invisible.
4. Tape a purple crayon inside and write in purple "To find out about the party, color this page with Harold's purple crayon."
5. Mail the invitation in a purple envelope.

Costumes

Ask guests to come dressed all in purple or give them purple T-shirts when they arrive. Or turn the guests into purple crayons. Wrap purple cloth around each guest and pin it in the back. Use purple party hats as crayon tips. (Or make your own hats. Roll and tape purple construction paper into cones and attach elastic bands.)

Decorations

- Make giant purple crayons from poster board. Hang them from the ceiling and tape them to the walls and door.
- Cover the walls with purple crepe paper and drape purple streamers from the center of the ceiling to the walls.
- Place purple balloons around the room.
- Set the table with a purple table-cloth and purple paper tableware. Set out white place mats with purple crayons for coloring.

Games

Purple Pictionary

Glue pictures of familiar items, such as a dog, toy, ball, house, pizza, and so on, onto index cards. Set a sketch pad on an easel. Give the first player a purple crayon and have her select a card. She must look at the card and then draw the item on the paper for the others to see. The first player to guess the item gets a point. Continue until everyone has drawn a picture. Award a prize to the player with the most points.

Purple Panic!

On each of several index cards, draw a circle and fill it in with a different color. Make extra purple cards. Stack the cards facedown in a pile. Place purple items around the room—some in plain sight, others more hidden but still visible. Have a player turn over a card. If the card is not purple, he gets to relax. If it is purple, he has thirty seconds to find something purple in the room. If he does, he remains in the game. If he doesn't, he's out. Repeat for each player. Tell the players they cannot choose a purple item that has already been found, so the game becomes more and more difficult. Continue playing until there is only one player left. Award that player a prize.

Prizes and Favors

- *Harold and the Purple Crayon* by Crockett Johnson
- Crayons
- Purple markers
- Purple paper
- Purple balloons

Activities

Purple Adventures

Give all the guests white paper and a purple crayon. Read one of Harold's purple crayon adventures. Have the kids pretend they are Harold. Ask them to draw what happens in the story. Have the kids take turns making up their own adventures for the others to draw.

Purple Dragon Art

Give the kids white paper and purple craft supplies, such as paint, crayons, markers, glitter, sequins, and crepe paper. Have them draw and decorate a purple dragon. In another room, tape the pictures under a sign that reads "Welcome to the Purple Dragon Gallery." Host a gallery opening and have the kids vote for the dragon that is the scariest, the funniest, the silliest, the sweetest, and so on.

Purple Pudding Magic

Place a few drops of purple food coloring in the bottom of a bowl, one for each child. (If purple food coloring is not available, combine red and blue food coloring.) Place vanilla pudding on top of the food coloring. Do not stir. Tell the kids you have cast a magic spell that will allow them to turn their white pudding purple. Ask them to stir the pudding.

Refreshments

- Plum pie
- Purple Cake: Tint white cake batter purple with a few drops of food coloring. Make purple frosting as well.
- Sandwiches with grape jelly
- Grape juice

If You Give a Mouse a Cookie

That mouse! All he wants is a cookie, and look what happens! The same thing could happen to you at your *If You Give a Mouse a Cookie* party if you don't watch out. So bring on the cookies!

Invitation

Mouse Cookie

1. Roll out ¼-inch-thick sugar cookie dough.
2. Cut the dough into a mouse head using a cookie cutter or knife. Don't make the ears too large, or they'll break off.
3. Bake the cookies according to package directions.
4. Just after they come out of the oven, insert a tongue depressor into the bottom of each head. Let the cookies cool.
5. Use tube frosting to decorate each cookie with eyes, nose, mouth, and whiskers.
6. Write the party details on a recipe card and punch a hole in one corner.
7. Tie the recipe card to the cookie stick.
8. Hand-deliver the invitation.

Variation: Draw a mouse head on folded brown construction paper. Make sure the tops of the ears are on the fold. Cut out the mouse head, leaving the fold intact. Add mouse details (eyes, nose, and so on) to the front and write the party details inside.

Costumes

Invite your guests to come dressed as the mouse in the book. Or when they arrive, give them mouse ears made out of stiff gray felt or gray craft foam attached to headbands. Make mouse

tails using rope or gray fake fur. Use face paints or eyebrow pencils to add noses and whiskers to the guests' faces.

Decorations

- Hang a "Mouse House" sign above your entryway.
- Make giant squares of Swiss cheese from large boxes painted yellow or orange. Cut holes out of the boxes or draw them using black paint or markers.

- Set out items mentioned in the book, such as an empty carton of milk, straws, napkins, mirrors, brooms, and so on. Don't forget the cookies!
- For added fun, draw the items as large as possible on paper or boxes so the kids feel small like mice.
- Make giant chocolate chip cookies from construction paper and hang them from the ceiling, use them as place mats, or tape them to the walls.

Games

Hidden Items

Collect all the items mentioned in the book or glue cut-out pictures of them onto cardboard. Hide the items or cutouts around the room. Read the story to the players and as you mention one of the items, have the kids race to find it. Keep reading until the book is finished and all the items are found. Award a prize to the player with the most items.

Floor Sweep

Divide the players into two teams and line them up on one side of the room. Put the same number of cotton balls in front of each team. Give the first players brooms. At the word "Go!" have them sweep all their cotton balls across the room. They then must race back and hand the brooms to the next teammates, who must race to the other side and sweep the cotton balls

Prizes and Favors

- *If You Give a Mouse a Cookie* by Laura Joffe Numeroff
- Toy mice
- Yellow shirts with a mouse decal in the middle
- Paper and crayons or markers

back to their teams. Continue sweeping back and forth until every player has had a turn. The team that finishes the race first wins a prize.

Activities

Mouse Cookies

Roll out sugar cookie dough. Let the kids cut out mice with cookie cutters. Bake the cookies according to package directions and allow them to cool. Have the kids decorate the cookies with frosting and candy decorations. Eat the cookies with milk!

Mouse Illustrations

Give the kids paper and crayons and ask them to illustrate the story as you read it out loud. When the story is finished, show off the pictures. Or have each guest draw the mouse in a new adventure. Ask a guest to hold up his picture and tell a story about what's happening. Have a second player hold up her picture and incorporate her drawing into the tale. Continue until everyone has had a turn telling part of the story.

Refreshments

- Cheese and crackers
- Cheese sandwiches
- Mouse Cake: Pour half of a batch of cake batter into a round cake pan. Pour the rest into 3 cupcake papers. Bake according to package directions but check the cakes early and insert a toothpick to see if they are done. Allow them to cool then assemble the mouse. Place the cake in the center of a plate. Place a cupcake in the middle of the cake to make a snout. Place the other cupcakes at the upper edge of the cake to make ears. Frost the entire cake white or chocolate. Draw a mouth with frosting and make whiskers with thin licorice strings. Make eyes with red-hots.

Lilly's Purple Plastic Purse

Howdy! Reach into your purple plastic purse and pull out a party for Lilly, who likes to draw, dance, write stories, and show her wonderful treasures. We'll visit Mr. Slinger's special classroom and share some fun together.

Invitation

Purple Purse

1. Cut 2 purses from purple plastic, felt, or construction paper.
2. Glue together the sides of the purse, leaving the top open.
3. Attach purple yarn or cord to each side of the purse to make straps.
4. Cut sunglasses from purple paper.
5. Write "Come to Lilly's Purple Plastic Purse Party!" and the party details on the glasses. Insert them into the purse.
6. Add 3 quarters or 3 silver play coins to the purse.

Costumes

Ask guests to come dressed all in purple or come dressed as Lilly. When they arrive, attach tails made from cord or rope and tie red bows at the ends. Have an adult dress as Mr. Slinger.

Decorations

- Tape ABC cutouts, educational posters, and photos of the guests to the wall.

- Set up a chalkboard and bulletin board.
- Line up rows of chairs and place paper and pens on the seats. Set a big table in the front for Mr. Slinger's desk. Place apples on the desk.
- Attach a "Lightbulb Lab—Where Great Ideas are Born" sign to a table. Hang a lightbulb from the ceiling directly overhead. Place paper and art supplies on the table for activity time.

Games

Interpretive Dances

Glue pictures of animals, actions, or sports onto index cards and place them facedown in a pile. Let each player choose a card. Turn on some children's or classical music and ask the first player to do an interpretive dance to express the picture. Have the other players guess what picture she has. The player who correctly guesses the most pictures wins a prize.

Draw-and-Guess

Write the guests' names on index cards and place them facedown in a pile. Give the players paper and markers. Have the kids each pick a card and draw a picture of that guest. When everyone is finished, hold up the pictures and let everyone guess who's who. You should have some funny pictures! The player who correctly identifies the most pictures wins a prize.

Favors

- *Lilly's Purple Plastic Purse* by Kevin Henkes
- Art supplies
- Purple light bulbs
- Purple stickers

Activities

Movie Star Sunglasses

Give each guest sunglasses and decorating supplies, such as sequins, glitter, permanent markers, trim, decals, feathers, sparkly pipe cleaners, and glue. Let the guests turn their plain sunglasses into Movie Star Sunglasses. Tie thin gold cord to the ends of the glasses so the guests can wear them around their necks.

Purple Plastic Purses

Let the kids decorate clear plastic makeup purses with purple markers, puffy paints, and fabric paints. Fill the purses with purple lip-gloss, eyeshadow, and other cosmetics.

Mr. Slinger's Shirts

Ask the guests to bring white T-shirts or provide them yourself. Let the kids decorate the shirts with fabric paints, puffy paints, or permanent markers. When the shirts are dry, have the guests wear them for the remainder of the party.

When I Grow Up

Provide hats for all types of careers, such as firefighter, detective, soldier, chef, doctor, artist, and so on. Set out a mirror. Let the guests try on the hats and talk about what they want to be when they grow up.

Refreshments

- Curly, crunchy, cheesy snacks
- Fish sticks
- Chocolate milk with a straw
- Cheese and crackers
- Purple Cake: Tint white cake batter purple with a few drops of food coloring. Make purple frosting as well.

The Lion King

Let's have a *hakuna matata* party and celebrate the story of Simba the Lion King. We'll have some adventures at Pride Rock; meet hyenas, wildebeests, meerkats, and wart hogs; and save the kingdom from Scar's terrible rule.

Invitation

Circle of Life

1. Cut a large circle from yellow construction paper and a small circle from orange construction paper.
2. Cut out a circle about the size of a silver dollar near the edge of the orange circle.
3. Place the orange circle on top of the yellow circle and attach them together in the center with a paper fastener so the circles can rotate.
4. Write "Circle of Life" on the orange circle. Write "Rotate yellow circle" with an arrow pointing in the correct direction under the round "window."
5. In the yellow area showing through the window, write some of the party details.
6. Rotate the yellow circle. Write more party details on the new area showing through the window.
7. Repeat until you've written all the party details.
8. Decorate the orange circle with pictures of Lion King characters and speech balloons that read "Come to a Lion King Party!"

Costumes

Ask your guests to come dressed as characters from the book. Add animal accessories when they arrive, such as ears, tails, noses, and paws. Make ears using stiff felt or craft foam attached to headbands. Make tails

from rope or fake fur. Use mittens for paws. Paint animal faces on the kids using face paint or eyebrow pencils.

Decorations

- Paint large boxes gray and brown to make rocks and caves.
- Drape the walls and ceiling with green streamers to create jungle vines.
- Hang toy birds from the ceiling.
- Tape posters of Africa to the walls. (You can often get these posters from a travel agency.)

- Tape pictures of wild animals to the walls.
- Set out stuffed animals.

Games

Mystery Animals

Pin a picture of an animal to the back of each player without letting him see the picture. Have one player show his back to everyone. Have the other players give one clue at a time, such as "You have soft fur," "You have a long tail," "You have stripes," "You have hooves," and so on. After each clue,

let the player guess what animal he is. Each time he guesses incorrectly, he gets another clue. When he guesses correctly, he wins a prize.

Save Simba

Set up obstacles in the party room and name them after things in the jungle, such as a rock, snake, jungle animal, river, quicksand, and so on. Set a stuffed lion on the other side of the room, beyond the obstacles. Tell the players to look carefully at the obstacle course. Then blindfold one player and have her walk to the other side of the room, retrieve the stuffed lion, and return, without falling into the quicksand, bumping into the rock, getting bitten by the snake, and so on. Ask the other kids to call out directions, such as "Move left two steps" or "Take a big step back." If the player safely returns with the lion, she wins a prize. If she doesn't, she must try again. If she still doesn't make it, she gets a funny booby prize. When it's the next player's turn, rearrange the obstacles.

Prizes and Favors
- *Disney's The Lion King* storybook
- Toy jungle animals
- Animal posters
- Animal coloring books

Listen to the Animals

Give a picture of an animal to each player. Have each player make the sound of the animal in the picture. Have the others guess what the animal is. The player who correctly identifies the most sounds wins a prize.

Activities

Animal Prints

Using a book of animals and their paw prints, photocopy an animal for each guest. Give the guests white construction paper and pour a variety of poster paints into saucers. Have the kids fingerpaint paw prints for their animals. When they're finished, ask everyone to guess what animal belongs to each set of paw prints. Some of these might be funny! Show the actual paw prints and compare them to the finger paintings.

Animal Masks

Make a mask for each guest by cutting eye and mouth holes out of a paper plate. Poke a small hole on each side of the plate and tie the ends of elastic thread (long enough to fit around a guest's head) to the holes. Let the kids make animal faces on their plates using decorating supplies, such as paint, markers, glitter, feathers, fabric pieces, and glue. When they're finished, ask them to put on their masks so you can have a parade. Videotape the parade and show the video during the party.

Refreshments

- Gummi worms
- Fruits, nuts, and seeds
- Peanut-butter-and-banana sandwiches
- Jungle Cake: Frost a sheet cake with chocolate frosting. Add green-tinted coconut for jungle grass. Set tiny plastic trees and animals on the cake.

The Little Engine That Could

I think we can... I think we can... have a *Little Engine That Could* party. All we have to do is decorate the party room, plan the games and activities, prepare the snacks, and hop on board the Little Blue Engine!

Invitation

Little Blue Engine

1. Draw the Little Blue Engine on blue construction paper and cut it out.
2. Fold white paper in half and glue the train inside.
3. Glue on white cotton balls for puffs of smoke.
4. On the front write "I think I can . . . I think I can . . . I think I can . . ."
5. Inside write "...have a Little Engine That Could Party!" Write the rest of the party details below the train.

Costumes

Ask your guests to come dressed as train engineers. Provide accessories, such as bandannas and caps. Or ask guests to come dressed as characters from the book, such as a clown, doll, teddy bear, Humpty Dumpty, or even a train.

Decorations

- Paint several large boxes to look like open train cars and others to look like boxcars. Remember to make the engine blue and the caboose red. Put the boxes next to one another to form a winding train.
- Make more train engines from smaller boxes and label them "Strong Engine," "Freight Engine,"

and "Rusty Old Engine." Place toys in them.

- Decorate the rest of the party room with colorful streamers and balloons.

Games

Train Race

Cut the bottoms and tops off of several large boxes (one for each child if possible). Ask each player to step inside a box, hold it around her waist, and pretend she is a train. Line up the "trains" on one side of the room or yard. At the word "Go!" have the trains race. The first one to reach the other side wins a prize. Have them race again, but make it more difficult by having them race sideways, backward, and so on.

Mailbag Relay

Find two bags to use as train mailbags. Line up the players in two teams. Place the mailbags at the opposite end of the room. At the word "Go!" the first players must run to their mailbags,

grab them, and carry them back to their teams. The next teammates must run the bags to the opposite side of the room, drop them, run back to their teams, and high-five the next

teammates, who run to pick up the bags again. The first team to finish the relay wins a prize.

Toy Touch

Place toys separately in paper bags. Pass a bag to the first player. Ask her to feel the toy in the bag and guess what it is. Have her look inside the bag without showing anyone else. If she's correct, she keeps the toy and drops out of the game. If she's wrong, she must pass the bag to the next player and let him guess. Continue until all the toys have been distributed.

Prizes and Favors
- *The Little Engine That Could* by Watty Piper
- Toy trains
- Toy clowns, dolls, teddy bears, airplanes, puzzles, and so on
- Train flags

Activities

Train Cars

Paint shoeboxes several different colors and detail them to look like train cars. Let each guest choose a train car and let her decorate it using markers, stickers, crepe paper, glue, scissors, magazine pictures, and so on. Line up the cars to make a train, fill each with a special snack, then let the kids take them home.

Free Spirit Picnic

Give everyone bandannas and yardsticks. Set out bagged sandwiches, fruit, packaged cookies, and small cartons of juice. Let the kids select the food they want to eat. Have them wrap their lunches in their bandannas. Tie the bandannas to the yardsticks and have the kids hoist their sticks over their shoulders. Take a walk to the nearest park and have a picnic lunch.

Refreshments

- Peppermint drops and lollipops
- Train Cake: Let the kids frost small loaves of banana bread different colors. Let them decorate the "train cars" with frosting, candies, sprinkles, and so on. Line up the loaves like a train then eat them.

Mother Goose

When you host a *Mother Goose* party, all kinds of interesting characters drop by: Jack Sprat and his wife, Little Miss Muffet and the spider, Mary with her lamb, and Little Jack Horner over in the corner. Let's celebrate Mother Goose's classic nursery rhymes.

Invitation

Hickory Dickory Clock

1. Cut a round clock from poster board.
2. Draw on the clock numbers.
3. Add hands pointing to the time of the party.
4. Around the dial, write a poem inviting the guests to the party, such as "Hickory Dickory Dock, the party's at ten o'clock. So dress up nice and join us mice until it's two o'clock!"
5. Mail the clock invitation along with a tiny toy mouse.

Costumes

Welcome the guests dressed as Mother Goose, wearing a bonnet, ruffled apron, and wire-rimmed glasses. Ask your guests to come dressed as Mother Goose characters, such as Wee Willie Winkie, Little Bo-Peep, the Three Blind Mice, and so on. Or assign costumes as your guests arrive, offering them nursery rhyme accessories, such as wire-rimmed glasses, pointy hats, caps, bonnets, aprons, pointy slippers, over-size shoes, vests, capes, and wigs.

Decorations

• Welcome the guests with a giant Mother Goose poster. Copy and color a large drawing of Mother Goose onto poster board. Embellish

the poster by gluing on fabric scraps, sequins, glitter, and trim.

- Write and illustrate nursery rhymes on poster board. Tape them to the walls.
- Photocopy pictures from Mother Goose books and glue them onto sturdy backing. Write the guests' names on them and use them as place cards.
- Using a large box, create a giant shoe for the Old Woman Who Lived in a Shoe, a crooked house for The Crooked Man, a tub for the Three Men in a Tub, or a pumpkin for Peter, Peter, Pumpkin Eater. Paint the box, detail it, and let the kids play inside.
- Set out stuffed animals and dolls representing Mother Goose characters, such as a lamb for Mary, a spider for Miss Muffet, a mouse for the Three Blind Mice, and so on.
- Hang spider webs for Miss Muffet, set out pumpkins for Peter, Peter, Pumpkin Eater, and put out shoes for the Old Woman Who Lived in a Shoe.

Games

Mystery Rhymes

Photocopy a Mother Goose nursery rhyme for each player. Pass out paper and markers. Have the players draw pictures to illustrate their nursery rhymes. When everyone is finished, hold up the pictures one at a time and let the other players guess the rhyme. Or have the players act out their nursery rhymes while the others guess. The player who correctly guesses the most rhymes wins a prize.

Escape the Pumpkin

Have players form a "pumpkin shell" by holding hands in a circle. One player stands inside the circle and tries to escape to the outside. Have the kids chant "Peter, Peter, Pumpkin Eater" while they play. If the trapped player breaks free, she wins a prize.

Spider Scare

Hide a big plastic spider and have players try to find it. Have them recite "Little Miss Muffet" as they search.

Prizes and Favors

- A collection of Mother Goose rhymes
- Toy Mother Goose characters
- Mother Goose coloring books
- Mother Goose rhymes on CD or cassette

The first player to find the spider wins a prize and gets to hide it again for the other players.

Activities

King and Queen of Hearts

Measure the circumference of each guest's head. Cut crowns from poster board based on the measurements. Do not tape the crowns closed. Lay the crowns flat and spray-paint them gold. Allow them to dry. Let the kids decorate their crowns using glitter, stickers, sequins, jewels, gold and silver trim, beads, feathers, scissors, tape, glue, markers, and so on. When the crowns are finished, wrap them around the guests' heads and tape them closed.

Mother Goofed!

Read out loud some popular nursery rhymes to the kids. Change the words as you read. For example, "Mary had a little goat." Pause after a mistake and let the kids call out the right word.

Jump Over Jack

Set an unlit taper candle in a candlestick on the floor. Clear plenty of space around the candle. Have the kids jump over the candle, trying not to get "burned" or knock the candle over. Ask the kids to recite "Jack Be Nimble" as they jump.

Refreshments

- Pumpkin custards for Peter, Peter Pumpkin Eater
- Heart-shaped cookies decorated with red icing for the Queen of Hearts
- Plums for Little Jack Horner
- Hard-boiled eggs for Humpty Dumpty
- Muffins for the Muffin Man

The Snowy Day

Create a winter wonderland for your *Snowy Day* party. Set up your indoor blizzard with lots of snow and ice, have some frosty fun and games, eat a few frozen treats, and collect warm memories of a cool time!

Invitation

Snowflake

1. Cut a large circle from white paper.
2. Fold it in half and then in half again.
3. Make triangle-shaped cuts or rounded cuts all along the edges to create snowflake designs.
4. Write party details on one side of the snowflake.

Costumes

Ask the guests to come dressed like Peter or dressed in snowsuits, ski clothes, or anything warm. Have extra mittens, hats, and earmuffs for those who forget the accessories. Or suggest that guests come dressed all in white like snowmen.

Decorations

- Place cotton balls, cotton batting, white doilies, snowflake cutouts, and white fabric around the room.
- Hang icicle lights from the ceiling.
- Fill the room with white balloons and hang white streamers from the ceiling.
- Cover the windows with "frost" that comes in a spray can.

• Spread a white tablecloth on the table and use white doilies as place mats.

Games

Snowsuit Relay

Divide the players into two teams. Set out two sets of adult-size winter outerwear, including snowsuits, hats, boots, mittens, and lots of scarves.

Have the players in each team race to put on and take off every item as fast as they can. The first team to finish the relay wins a prize.

Ice Cube Toss

Pair the players and have them wear mittens. Give each pair an ice cube. Have the players in each pair stand a few feet apart and toss the ice cube back and forth. Each time one catches

the cube, both must take a step back. If one drops the cube, the pair is out of the game. The last pair remaining wins a prize.

Prizes and Favors

- *The Snowy Day* by Ezra Jack Keats
- Plastic bags filled with marshmallows and tied with ribbon (Attach a card that reads "Snowman Droppings" for a great laugh.)
- Decorative wool socks
- Hot chocolate packets, mini marshmallows, and mugs
- Toy polar bears or penguins

Mitten Relay

Divide the players into two teams. Give each player a pair of mittens and set a bowl of unwrapped bubble gum pieces between the two teams. With their mittens on, the first players must each grab a piece of bubble gum, unwrap it, stick it their mouths, and high-five the next teammates in line. These players then repeat the tasks. The first team to complete the relay wins a prize.

Snowball Race

Divide the players into two teams. Give the first players a large spoon with a cotton "snowball" balanced on it. Players must race from one side of the room to the other without losing the snowball. If a player drops a snowball, she must start over. The first team to finish the relay wins a prize.

Activities

Snow World

Have the kids build snowmen, snow cars, and snow houses with marshmallows and toothpicks. Let them use toothpicks to paint the marshmallows with food coloring. Then melt some marshmallows and make Rice Krispies Treats.

Go Outside!

Bundle up all the guests and enjoy real snow outside. Make snow angels. Put tinted water in squirt bottles and let the kids draw pictures on the snow. Before the party, freeze tinted water in clean milk cartons, ice cube trays, yogurt containers, and so on. Have the kids build snow castles and give them the tinted ice to use as decorations. (If there's no snow outside,

clear any breakables from the room, give the kids wadded white socks, and let them have a "snowball" fight!)

Refreshments

- Snowball Cake: Bake cake batter according to package directions in a well-greased ovenproof bowl. Frost the cake white and sprinkle coconut on it.
- Let the kids frost cupcakes white and sprinkle coconut on them.
- Hot chocolate with marshmallows, whipped cream, and a candy cane stirrer
- Let the kids decorate sugar cookie snowmen.
- Frozen Banana Pops: Cut bananas in half and insert a tongue depressor into the bottom of each half. Freeze the bananas and then serve them.
- Make slushies by blending ice cubes with fruit syrup or frozen strawberries.

The Three Little Pigs

We promise by the hairs of our chinny-chin-chins that you'll have a houseful of fun at our *Three Little Pigs* party. We'll try to keep the Big Bad Wolf away!

Invitation

House Made of Brick

1. Make 2 "front doors" by folding the sides of red construction paper to meet in the middle.
2. Draw horizontal and vertical lines on the front to make it look as if it were made of brick.
3. Open the doors and glue a picture of the Three Little Pigs inside.
4. Write the party details on the insides of the doors, including a quotation from the book.
5. Write "The Three Little Pigs" as the return address.

Costumes

Invite guests to come dressed all in pink. When they arrive, give them pig snouts made from pink poster board. Draw two black dots for nostrils and attach the ends of elastic string (long

enough to fit around a guest's head) to each side. Make curly pink tails by twisting a pipe cleaner around a pencil. Attach the tails to the kids' clothing with duct tape or wrap the ends of the pipe cleaners around belt loops. Rent a wolf costume for an adult to wear. Have the adult surprise the kids during the party.

Decorations

- Paint a large box yellow to look like a straw house. Glue some tufts of straw onto the outside. Cut a large

door so the kids can easily get inside and out.

- Paint a second box to look like a stick house. Glue a few real twigs onto the outside. Cut a large door so the kids can easily get inside and out.
- Paint a third box to look like a brick house. Stack real bricks at the base of the house. Cut a large door so the kids can easily get inside and out.
- Cut a large tree trunk from brown construction paper. Cut leaves from green construction paper. Tape the

tree to a wall. Have a wolf nose peeking from behind the tree.

Games

Let Me In!

Choose one player to be the wolf and tell the rest they are the pigs. Have the pigs stand in the straw house. The wolf says, "Little pig, little pig, let me in!" The pigs answer, "Not by the hair of my chinny-chin-chin!" The wolf says, "Then I'll huff and I'll puff and I'll blow your house in!" At this point, the pigs must run to the safety of the stick

house without being tagged by the wolf. If the wolf tags a pig, the pig becomes a wolf, too. Repeat so the pigs run to the brick house, back to the straw house, and so on. Keep playing until one pig remains untagged (award that player a prize) or until the wolves and pigs huff and puff from exhaustion.

Huff and Puff

Line the kids on all fours across the floor. Tape a line in front of them and another several feet across the room. Place a cotton ball in front of each player. At the words "Huff and puff!" have them blow the cotton balls across the floor. The first player to blow his cotton ball across the finish line wins a prize.

Activities

Mini Pig Houses

Have the kids make houses for the Three Little Pigs using small boxes. Provide paint, markers, glitter, and other supplies to decorate the houses. Give the kids little plastic pigs to put inside their completed houses.

Favors and Prizes
- *The Three Little Pigs*
- Toy pigs or wolves
- Posters of pigs or wolves

Pig and Wolf Masks

Make a mask for each guest by cutting eye and mouth holes out of a paper plate. Poke a small hole on each side of the plate and tie the ends of elastic string (long enough to fit around a guest's head) to the holes. Have the kids decorate the masks using pink or brown paint, markers, glitter, and so on.

Refreshments

- Buy premade pigs in a blanket or make your own by wrapping cocktail wieners in refrigerated biscuit dough. Bake according to package directions and serve with mustard or ketchup.

- Corn on the cob
- Heat up a favorite soup and call it "Wolf Soup."
- Haystacks: Spoon crumbled Shredded Wheat biscuits onto a baking sheet and sprinkle the mounds with cheese. Broil until the cheese melts.
- Piggy Punch with Curly Tails: Tint milk pink with a few drops of red food coloring and serve with a crazy straw that looks like a pig's tail.

The Very Hungry Caterpillar

Caterpillars aren't the only ones who get hungry . . . so do kids! So make sure there is a lot of tasty food at your *Very Hungry Caterpillar* party. If you are lucky, the food will change your guests from crawly caterpillars to beautiful butterflies!

Invitation

Cocoon Surprise

1. Draw the outline of a butterfly on white paper.
2. Write the party details inside the wings.
3. Cut out the butterfly.
4. Paint or color the front with bright colors. Paint or color the back brown.
5. Roll the butterfly with the brown side facing out to look like a cocoon.
6. Insert the "cocoon" into an envelope. When a guest unrolls the cocoon, he'll find the beautiful butterfly inside.

Costumes

Suggest that guests come dressed as butterflies, caterpillars, or cocoons. Add accessories when they arrive, such as antennae headbands made from small, colored Styrofoam balls stuck onto sparkly pipe cleaners. Pin crepe paper wings to the butterfly guests' backs.

Decorations

- Tape pictures of butterflies to the walls and hang them from the ceiling.
- Make giant butterflies and caterpillars from white construction paper. Decorate them and tape them to the door.
- Tape pictures of the foods the caterpillar eats to the walls.
- Place the real food items on the table as a centerpiece along with a stuffed caterpillar or butterfly.

- Place toy caterpillars and butterflies around the room and on the table.
- Tape a tree made from green and brown construction paper to the wall. Attach paper butterflies to the leaves, cocoons to the branches, and caterpillars to the trunk.

Games

Caterpillar Crawl

Cut openings at both ends of boxes large enough for kids to crawl through. Paint the boxes to look like the foods the caterpillar eats. Make two tunnels

of end-to-end boxes. Divide the players into two teams and have them crawl through the boxes like caterpillars. The first team to have all its players crawl through its tunnel wins a prize.

Caterpillar Hunt

Make fuzzy caterpillars from pipe cleaners and pompoms. Hide them throughout the party room. Have the kids hunt for the caterpillars. The player with the most caterpillars wins a prize.

Prizes and Favors
- *The Very Hungry Caterpillar* by Eric Carle
- Toy caterpillars or butterflies
- Insect books

Caterpillar Taste Test

Cut up pieces of the foods mentioned in the book. Blindfold one player. Offer her a piece of the food and have her guess what it is. Make sure each guest has a turn at the taste test. The player who correctly identifies the most food wins a prize.

Activities

Caterpillars

Help the kids make caterpillars by gluing green pompoms onto green pipe cleaners. Add googly eyes to a red pompom to make a face. Give the kids squares of green felt to use as foundations for their caterpillars.

Butterflies

Give the kids poster paints and white paper and let them paint freeform. Sprinkle the wet paint with glitter. Allow the paper to dry then cut out butterflies. Create cocoons by covering cardboard tubes with green crepe paper. Roll the butterflies and place them each inside a cocoon. Let the kids take the cocoons home and decide when they want their butterflies to emerge.

Butterfly Cookies

Bake butter cookies in the shape of butterflies. (Use a butterfly-shaped cookie cutter or a knife.) Let the kids decorate the butterflies with frosting, sprinkles, and so on.

Refreshments

- Fruit salad with apples, pears, plums, strawberries, and oranges
- Strawberries and cream
- Chocolate cake
- Ice-cream cones
- Pickles
- Swiss cheese and salami sandwiches
- Lollipops
- Cherry pie
- Sausages
- Watermelon
- Frost cupcakes green and set them in a row to create a long caterpillar. Decorate the first cupcake to look like a face.

Where the Wild Things Are

Be king or queen of the jungle at a wild rumpus with Max and the Wild Things. We'll have a wild time in our wolf suits until we sail back home— where supper will still be waiting!

Invitation

Max's Private Boat

1. Fold brown construction paper in half.
2. Draw the outline of a boat with its bottom on the fold.
3. Cut out the boat, leaving the fold intact.
4. Open the boat and glue a picture of Max or a Wild Thing inside. Make sure that the head peeks out when the card is closed.
5. Write the party details below the picture.

Costumes

Ask guests to come dressed as Max. Offer the guests Max's wolf ears made from fake fur attached to headbands, tails made from rope, or pointy crowns made from gold poster board

and decorated with glued-on jewels. Or ask guests to come dressed as Wild Things. Offer Wild Thing ears, claws, false teeth, hairy wigs, and so on.

Decorations

- Tape construction paper palm trees to the walls. Hang streamers from the ceiling to create vines.
- Cover the table with jungle-print fabric or a green tablecloth. Cut giant

leaves from green construction paper for place mats.

- Tape blue construction or crepe paper around the base of the walls to create an ocean.
- Draw giant Wild Things on poster board, cut them out, and tape them to the walls.

Games

Wild Rumpus

Gather the Wild Things in a circle and tell them not to move a muscle. When you turn on the "rumpus" music, the Wild Things must go wild and dance around in a frenzy! But the minute the music stops, the Wild Things must be still. If a Wild Thing loses his balance and falls or moves, he's out of the

game. Continue until there's only one Wild Thing left and award her a prize.

Staring Contest

Choose two players to have a staring contest. The first one to blink loses. The player who doesn't blink goes on to stare at another player. The staring champion wins a prize.

Prizes and Favors

- *Where the Wild Things Are* by Maurice Sendak
- Max or Wild Things toys
- Toy wolves
- Toy boats

Activities

Wild Thing Masks

Make a mask for each guest by cutting eye and mouth holes out of a paper plate. Poke a small hole on each side of the plate and tie the ends of elastic string (long enough to fit around a guest's head) to the holes. Have the kids make Wild Thing masks using markers, feathers, glitter, fake fur, and so on. Have them put on the masks and then have a wild rumpus. Videotape the rumpus and show the video during the party.

Magical Boats

Give the kids boxes large enough for them to sit in. Provide paint, markers, stickers, colored tape, and other items and have the kids decorate their "boats." When the boats are finished, make believe you're sailing to the island to meet the Wild Things.

Hoist the Flag!

Cut out rectangles from white cotton fabric. Buy three-foot-long dowels and staple the fabric onto each one to make a flag. Let the kids decorate their flags using markers, decals, fabric paints, and so on.

Refreshments

- Macaroni and cheese
- Tuna Boats: Hollow out green pepper halves and fill them with tuna salad. Make flags for the boats from cheese slices on toothpicks.
- Jungle Juice: Blend orange juice and bananas in a blender.
- Goldfish and animal crackers

Alice's Adventures in Wonderland

Alice has a puzzling time trying to keep up with the Hatter, the March Hare, and the very sleepy Dormouse. Host your own Wonderland party and see if you can solve the funny riddles and crazy games before things get curiouser and curiouser.

Invitation

The Queen of Hearts

1. Fold white construction paper in half.
2. Glue several heart playing cards onto the front.
3. In the form of a riddle, write a hint about the party under the cards, such as "Oh my ears and whiskers, it's time for Hatter's riddle: What has food and fun and games right in the middle?"
4. Write the answer—the party details —inside.

Costumes

Ask guests to come dressed as characters from the book: Alice, the Hatter, Queen of Hearts, White Rabbit, Cheshire Cat, Dormouse, and so on.

When they arrive, offer the guests accessories, such as aprons, construction paper stovepipe hats, heart-shaped stickers, eyebrow-penciled whiskers, or face paint.

Decorations

- Set up the Hatter's mad tea party on a long table covered with a tablecloth featuring hearts, playing cards, or polka dots.
- Place teacups, teapots, and tea bags on the table with "Drink Me" signs on them.

- Set out a small heart-shaped cake with an "Eat Me" sign for a centerpiece.
- Put a small rubber or stuffed mouse in a teapot. Make sure the mouse's head peeks out.
- Tie colorful balloons to the chair backs and hang streamers from the ceiling to the walls.
- Set out a vase filled with artificial or real roses.
- Make place cards from playing cards.

Games

Queen of Hearts Maze

Tie one end of a skein of red yarn to the front door. Then walk through various rooms and unwind the yarn, hooking it onto furniture, doorknobs, and so on. Also tie a skein of white yarn to the front door, but unwind it along a different path. Divide the players into Red and White teams and gather them at the door. Have the players follow their yarn paths, rolling up the yarn as they go. The first team to follow its

maze and return to the front door with a ball of yarn wins a prize.

Caucus Race

Have the players stand in a circle. Read the book out loud and tell the players they have to keep moving while you read. The moment you stop reading, everyone must stop moving. If a player moves, she's out of the

Prizes and Favors
- *Alice's Adventures in Wonderland* or *Through the Looking Glass* by Lewis Carroll
- Funny poetry and riddle books
- Decks of cards
- Paper roses

game. The last player left in the game wins a prize.

Dormouse Game

Give players paper and markers. One player chooses a letter of the alphabet. Everyone else must draw items that begin with the selected letter. For example, if the letter is M, the kids might draw a mousetrap, moon, magician, and so on. Let the players draw for one minute. The player who chose the letter should see who came up with the most items beginning with M. That player wins a prize. Take turns so everyone gets a chance to call out a letter.

Activities

Crazy Croquet

Give guests mallets. Plastic pink flamingos would be perfect. If you can't find flamingos, choose another unwieldy or funny object. Choose a soft ball that doesn't roll well, such as plastic netting stuffed with cotton. Have kids take turns being the wickets. Tell them to move around whenever they like (as the soldier-wickets did in the book) to make the game more challenging. Have the kids create the rest of the rules and then let them play!

Roses

At the beginning of the party, give the kids ceramic or plaster roses and let them paint them with acrylic paints. (It's important to do this activity early so the paint has time to dry properly.)

Mad Hats

Measure the circumference of each guest's head. Cut poster board into rectangles based on the measure- ments. Let the kids make their hats as mad as they like using bows, rib- bons, stickers, faux jewels, markers, paint, and so on. Glue the rectangles into cylinders and have the guests wear their mad hats.

Queen's Heart Cookies

Cut sugar cookie dough into hearts with a cookie cutter or a knife. For half of the cookies, cut out a small heart in the center. Bake the heart cutouts and the cookies. Spread strawberry or raspberry jam on the solid cookies and top them with the heart cutouts. Let the kids decorate the remaining cookies with sprinkles and red, pink, and white frosting.

Refreshments

- Fruity herbal teas
- Cupcakes
- Heart-shaped sandwiches
- Cheese

Amelia Bedelia

Amelia Bedelia is a crazy, mixed-up lady who has fun with the meanings of words. So why not have a mixed-up party to celebrate her crazy world? Just watch what you say—your words might come out mixed-up if you're not careful!

Invitation

Mixed-up Message

1. Fold construction paper in half.
2. Instead of writing the party details on the front, write them on the back. To make things even more mixed-up, write the party details backward: "!ytraP ailedeB ailemA na ot emoC."
3. Open the card from the back and write the rest of the party details inside, starting at the bottom of the page and moving up.
4. Write the party details as a to-do list.

Costumes

Ask the kids to come dressed as Amelia or provide them with aprons and feather dusters when they arrive. Tell your guests to do something crazy with their outfits, just like Amelia would, such as wear their socks over their shoes. Or give them accessories, such as hats, gloves, glasses, and so on, and let them think of crazy ways to wear them.

Decorations

- Greet your guests facing backward and tell them "not" to come in.
- Tape upside-down posters and pictures to the walls.

- Hang balloons by string from the ceiling so they appear upside down.
- Turn knickknacks in the party room upside down.
- Put place settings under the table and have the kids eat on the floor. (Make sure your table is high enough for them to sit comfortably. Also, of course, make sure the floor is very clean!)
- Look around the room for things you can mix up, overturn, or display backward.

Games

Double Meanings

On index cards, write common phrases that have double meanings, such as "Pick up your room," "Stop fiddling around," "Clean your plate," "Watch your step," and so on. Pass the cards to the players and have them take turns acting out the phrases literally. Have the other players try to guess the phrases. The player who identifies

the most phrases wins a prize. Have the kids write their own phrases with double meanings and play again.

What Does It Mean?

Pass out paper and pencils to the players. Have one player read a word that no one knows from the dictionary. Have that player write the real meaning of the word. Have the rest of the players each make up a meaning for the same word. Give all the words to the first player and have her read the meanings out loud. Have the rest of the group try to guess which meaning is correct. Award a point for every correct guess. The player with the most points wins a prize.

Favors and Prizes

- *Amelia Bedelia* or other books in the series by Peggy Parish
- Personalized aprons
- Packaged fruit pies
- Riddle books
- Tiny dictionaries
- Inside-out T-shirts

Activities

Don't Do It Right

On index cards, write some easy stunts, such as "Write the alphabet,"

"Draw a picture," "Put on your shoes," "Do a dance," "Walk around the room," "Sing a song," and so on. Have the first player choose a stunt to perform. The trick is he can't do it the right way—he must do it in a creative new way. For example, he might write the alphabet out of order, put his shoes on before his socks, and so on! Repeat until everyone has had a chance to do a stunt in a mixed-up way.

Bedelia Pie

Roll out pie dough to fit small pie pans, one for each guest. Have the kids wash their hands and put on aprons (backward, of course!). Read the first step in a simple pie recipe, but instead of reading it correctly, make a mistake, such as "Pour 4 cups of sugar into the sink." Let the cooks try to guess what's wrong with the instruction. When they've figured out the correct instruction, let them complete the step. Continue reading the instructions incorrectly, with the kids correcting them, until the pies are ready to bake.

Refreshments

- Upside-Down Sundaes: Place a cherry in a glass and top with nuts. Add whipped cream, then chocolate syrup, and finally ice cream.
- Milk in a wineglass, juice in a coffee mug, or soda in a bowl
- Inverted Sandwiches: Put a bread slice between 2 slices of cheese or meat.

Arthur's April Fool

Are you ready to have some foolish fun with your friends? Then join Arthur on April Fools' Day and have a tricky time!

Invitation

Puzzle

1. Write party details on black construction paper using glow-in-the-dark ink. Invite your guests to "Arthur's Greatest April Fools' Party on Earth!"
2. Decorate the card with pictures of Arthur. Draw on stars or decorate with star stickers.
3. Cut the card into puzzle pieces and place them in an envelope.
4. On the outside of the envelope, instruct the guest to assemble the puzzle and read the secret information in a dark room.
5. Include a practical joke in the envelope as well, such as pepper gum or a plastic spider.

Costumes

Have the kids come dressed as characters from an Arthur book. Or ask the kids to come dressed in jeans and a white shirt, then turn them into Arthur with large round glasses, red bow ties, and aardvark ears (made from stiff brown felt or brown craft foam attached to headbands) when they arrive. Give the kids costume accessories mentioned in the book, such as bloody fangs, purple wigs, huge dark glasses with red frames, wax lips, and so on.

Decorations

- Create Arthur's school auditorium, complete with a stage for Arthur and his friends to present their April Fools' Day gags. Place chairs around the stage. Make a stage curtain from yellow fabric or crepe paper.

- Cover the table with a blue paper tablecloth and use red, blue, and yellow place settings.
- Place wax lips, fake teeth, giant glasses, and other items at each place setting.
- Make a large sign that reads "Arthur's Greatest Tricks on Earth" and prop it on an easel near the stage.

Games

The Magician's Secret

Divide the players into two teams and have two adults each take a team into a separate room. Using a kids' magic book, have the adult teach each player a magic trick. When both teams have

Prizes and Favors

- *Arthur's April Fool* or other books in the series by Marc Brown
- Novelties, tricks, and jokes
- Joke books

learned their tricks, return to the party room and have the teams sit on opposite sides. Have one player from Team A perform a trick for Team B. After the trick is finished, Team B has two minutes to explain the trick. If they figure it out, they get a point. Have the players take turns performing tricks for the other team. The team with the most points wins a prize.

Punch Line

Write a joke on an index card, but write the punch line in parentheses. Have one player pick a card and read the joke but not the punch line. The first player to call out the punch line wins the card. Take turns until everyone has read a card. The player with the most cards wins a prize.

Activities

Amazing Mind Reading

Choose one guest to be the mind reader and teach her this trick before the party. Have the mind reader wear a towel turban and a robe covered with stick-on stars. Ask her to leave the room. Choose one player to point to an item in the room. Ask the mind reader to return and guess which item the player selected. She gets three guesses. Here's the trick: You, as moderator, ask the mind reader a question that begins with the first letter of the chosen item. For example, if a player chooses the cake, the question might be "Can you tell us what the item is?" If the mind reader guesses wrong the first time, begin another question with the second letter of the item, such as "Are you ready to try again?" The mind reader now has two letters to help her guess the object (c and a). If she still guesses wrong, ask a third question beginning with the third letter of the object.

Star Capes

Cut silky red fabric into capes. Let the kids glue paper stars to the capes or paint stars on them using fabric paint. Glow-in-the-dark paint is especially fun! Pin the capes to the kids' shoulders.

Refreshments

- Cheeseburgers
- Chocolate cream pie
- Oreo cookies
- Cinnamon candies
- Soda with a plastic ice cube with a bug in it

Babe: The Gallant Pig

Join in the farm fun at this *Babe* party. Let's visit Farmer Hogget and see what his animals are up to!

Invitation

Pink Pig Snout

1. Cut a circle about 2 inches in diameter from pink poster board.
2. Color two black dots in the middle to make a pig snout.
3. Make a hole on each side of the snout. Tie an end of elastic string to each hole so the snout can be worn on the face.
4. Write the party details on the back.
5. Mail the snout in an envelope filled with straw.

Costumes

Ask the kids to come dressed as farmers. Or have the kids come wearing their snout invitations and give them pig ears made from stiff pink felt or pink craft foam attached to headbands. Make pipe cleaner tails by curling pink pipe cleaners around a pencil. Attach the tails using duct tape or by wrapping the pipe cleaners around belt loops. Use face paints to transform the guests' faces into Babe's face.

Decorations

- Set out stuffed farm animals.
- Set a stuffed pig on the center of a red-and-white-checked tablecloth. Sprinkle hay and popcorn kernels on the table.
- Tape pictures of farms and animals to the walls.
- Play bluegrass music.

- Hang a dinner bell to ring at mealtime. (A triangle or wind chime will also work.)

Games

Grand Challenge Sheepdog Trials

Build an obstacle course and have the players take turns being Babe. Give the first player a stick and a ball. The ball represents a sheep. Have the player jump over hurdles, run around blockades, crawl through tunnels, and so on while "herding the sheep" (hitting the ball with the stick) along the way. Time each player. The fastest Babe wins a prize.

Animal Walk

Give each player an index card with a farm animal written on it. Have the players take turns walking like their assigned animals while the rest try to identify the animals. The "animals" are not allowed to make any noises.

The player who identifies the most animals wins a prize.

Paws Relay

Divide the players into two teams. Dig out all of Dad's clean socks and have each player put them on his hands to make paws. (If you don't have enough socks, give each team a pair and have the players take turns wearing the socks.) Set a bowl of unwrapped pieces of bubble gum between the two teams. At the word "Go!" the first players must grab a piece of bubble gum, unwrap it with their paws, stick it their mouths, and high-five the next teammates in line. These players must then repeat the tasks. The first team to complete the relay wins a prize.

Prizes and Favors

- *Babe: The Gallant Pig* by Dick King-Smith
- Toy pigs, dogs, or sheep
- Bandannas
- Farmer hats

Activities

Puffy Pig Refrigerator Magnets

Give each guest two pink pompoms, a piece of pink felt, two googly eyes, and a pink pipe cleaner. Set out pencils, scissors, glue, and a roll of magnetic tape. Have the kids follow these instructions: Place the pompoms close together on the felt and trace around them. Cut along the outline. Cut a short strip of magnetic tape, peel off the protective paper, and stick it onto one side of the felt cutout. On the other side, glue on the pompoms to make the pig's body. Cut out ears, feet, and snout from the leftover felt and glue them onto the pig. Glue on googly eyes. Curl a pipe cleaner to make a tail, add glue to one end, and stick it in between the pompom and felt. Let the pig dry then stick it to the refrigerator.

Farm Collages

Give the kids glue, paper, and farm-related items, such as hay, seeds, kernels, feathers, leaves, pebbles, twigs, and so on. Have them create a farm by gluing the items onto the paper.

Fruit and Veggie Prints

Slice different fruits and vegetables to expose the middles. Use apples, oranges, cucumbers, zucchini, bell peppers, kiwi fruit, and so on. Give each guest paper and a paintbrush. Tell the kids to paint the flat end of the fruits and veggies with poster paint and then press them onto the paper.

Refreshments

- Vegetables with dip
- Milk
- Shepherd's pie
- Taffy
- Caramel apples

The Jungle Book

Take a trip to the jungle with Mowgli, the wolf pack, and the rest of his animal friends. Don't worry about the snakes, bears, and panthers—they're friendly animals that call humans "frogs"!

Invitation

Mowgli's Jungle

1. Fold white construction paper in half and glue a picture of the jungle onto the front.
2. Write "Welcome to Mowgli's Jungle" below the picture.
3. Glue pictures of jungle animals inside.
4. Write the party details inside, weaving the words around the animals.
5. Sprinkle some grass or leaves in the envelope.

Costumes

Ask guests to come dressed as Mowgli or as animals featured in the story. Or ask guests to come dressed in safari clothes. Provide accessories, such as sun visors, toy binoculars, compasses, water canteens, and so on.

Decorations

- Drape green and brown streamers from the ceiling and walls to create jungle vines.
- Cover the furniture with animal-print fabric to make tigers, zebras, and ocelots.
- Make a pool by spreading blue fabric on the floor.
- Make quicksand by spreading brown fabric on the floor. Put a sign near it that reads "Danger! Quicksand!"

- Tape trees made from brown and green construction paper to the walls. Make three-dimensional trees using boxes painted brown and green. Add leaves made from green construction paper.
- Play a CD of jungle noises or the soundtrack from *The Jungle Book.*

Games

Run through the Jungle

Set up an obstacle course through the house or yard. Label the obstacles "Quicksand," "Watering Hole," "Snake Pit," "Wolf Den," and so on. Let the kids take turns being Mowgli. Time how fast each player runs through the jungle. The fastest Mowgli wins a prize.

Animals in the Bush

Glue pictures of jungle animals onto separate index cards and place them facedown in a pile. Have a player draw a card and act out the animal without making any noises. The first player to guess the animal wins a point. Keep playing until all the cards are used. Award a prize to the player with the most points.

Activities

Snake in the Grass

Have the kids change into their swim-suits. Lay a sprinkler hose on the lawn. Have one player turn the sprinkler on and off without looking at the other players. The other players must try to make it from one end of the lawn to the other without getting wet.

Jungle Path

Divide the guests into two teams. Put one team in the front yard and one in the back yard. Have each team hide a stuffed jungle animal and leave a trail for the other team to follow, using rocks, sticks, leaves, and so on. When the trails are ready, have the teams take turns following the clues to the animals.

Prizes and Favors

- *The Jungle Book* by Rudyard Kipling
- Toy jungle animals
- Animal coloring books

Hunt for Food

Package snacks in airtight containers. Hide them throughout the house or yard. Have the kids hunt for the food and bring it back to the table to share.

Refreshments

- Jungle mix (nuts, seeds, cereal, dried fruit, and so on)
- Edible flowers from a flower shop or a gourmet grocery store
- Serve chocolate milk and call it "panther's milk"
- Paw Print Cakes: Frost cupcakes with chocolate frosting and top each with three round, flat candies to make animal toe prints. Arrange the cupcakes on the table to make a trail of paw prints.
- Turtle chocolates

Little House on the Prairie

We're moving west for a *Little House on the Prairie* party. Join the three Ingalls girls—Mary, Laura, and Carrie—for a celebration of Founder's Day and life on the farm.

Invitation

Farmer's Handkerchief

1. Write the party details on a bandanna with either a washable or permanent marker.
2. Use "Little House on the Prairie" as the return address.

Costumes

Suggest that the girls come dressed in long summer dresses, aprons, and bonnets. If they have long hair, tell them to wear it in braids. Suggest that the boys come dressed in pants with suspenders, white shirts with collars, and wide-brimmed hats. Or have the guests come dressed as farmers and give them bandannas, hats, and gloves when they arrive.

Decorations

- Paint a large box to look like a little wooden farmhouse.
- Tape posters of the Old West, prairies, farmhouses, or big-sky landscapes to the walls.
- Add pictures of farm animals to the landscapes.
- Cover a picnic table with a checkered tablecloth and serve food from iron pots. Use camping plates and flatware and serve drinks in tin cups or jelly jars. Use bandannas as place mats.

- Fill a jelly jar with wildflowers for a centerpiece.
- Play square-dancing music and bluegrass tunes.

Games

Farmyard Freeze

Put on some bluegrass music and have the kids act out farm chores, such as milking a cow or hoeing a field. Every few minutes, stop the music. Everyone must freeze when the music stops. If anyone moves, he is out of the game. Keep playing until there's only one player left and award her a prize.

Founder's Day Games

Celebrate Founder's Day with many different games. Tug of war: Spread a brown towel on the floor for "mud" and place the teams at opposite ends of a rope. The team that pulls the other into the mud wins a prize. Jump rope contests: Award prizes to players who can jump the longest, do the most tricks, jump the fastest, and so on. Three-legged race: Have pairs stand side by side and have each player put

the leg next to her partner's leg inside a flour sack or pillowcase. Have them race from one end of the yard to the other. The fastest pair wins a prize. Pie-eating contest: Place small pies on a table covered with a plastic sheet.

Prizes and Favors

- *Little House on the Prairie* or other books in the series by Laura Ingalls Wilder
- Toy farm animals
- Books about pioneers
- Hair-braiding kits

Have the players put on smocks or aprons and have them keep their hands behind their backs. The first player to eat his whole pie wins a prize.

Activities

Jammin'

Provide each guest with a baby food or jam jar. Supply the guests with stickers, puffy paints, permanent markers, and fancy ribbons to decorate their jars. If you're holding the party during berry-picking time, make jam before the party or while the kids decorate their jars. Let the kids help you ladle jam into their jars to take home. Or have guests churn butter. Fill the jars about two-thirds full with whipping cream. Close the lids tightly and have guests shake the jars for about ten to fifteen minutes. The watery whey will separate from the butter. Pour it out, then serve the butter on homemade bread or muffins.

Slate Stories

Give each guest a slate and a piece of chalk. (If you can't find slates, use black construction paper.) Give the kids three minutes to draw a scene of the Old West. When time is up, have the kids sit in a circle and pass their slates to the guests on the right. Let them look at the pictures for a minute. Ask the first guest to show her friend's picture and tell a story about it for exactly one minute. At that time, the next guest has one minute to show his friend's picture and incorporate it into the story. Keep playing until everyone has had a turn telling part of the story.

Square Dancing

If possible, hire a caller to teach the kids how to square-dance. If not, turn on some lively music and let the kids create their own square dance moves. Have them take turns being the caller while the others dance.

Refreshments

- Pies
- Sandwiches made with homemade jam and butter
- Baked goods, such as muffins, breads, rolls, cookies, and so on
- Popovers or cream puffs filled with whipped cream, pudding, ice cream, or jam
- Homemade lemonade
- Pickles
- Blackberries and cream
- Maple syrup candy

Madeline

Take a trip to Paris with Madeline and share her adventures through rain or shine. We'll eat French food, play French games, and dress up as Madeline!

Invitation

Picture of Paris

1. Make a postcard using a white, unlined index card.
2. Draw a picture of the Eiffel Tower on the front and color it red and blue.
3. Write the party details on the back using French words in the text. For example, "Come to la fête de Madeline!"
4. Staple a ribbon like the one on Madeline's hat to the postcard.

Costumes

Ask the guests to come dressed as Madeline or Miss Clavel. Or have the guests wear berets to the party.

Decorations

- Tape posters of France to the walls. (You can get them at a travel agency.)
- Drape fake ivy from the ceiling to create the vine-covered house.
- Set out flowers, loaves of French bread, and fancy bottles of perfume—all in straight lines of course!
- Use a hat that looks like Madeline's as your centerpiece. Use small hats as place cards.
- Play French music.

Games

"Something Is Not Right!"

Set out groups of things that belong together, such as pictures of France,

lists of French words, a collection of French foods, and so on. To each group add one thing that doesn't belong, such as a picture of Mexico among the pictures of France, a Russian word among the French words, an egg roll among the French foods, and so on. Give the players pencils and paper and tell them "something is not right." Set a timer and give everyone two minutes to write down the item that doesn't belong in each group. When time is up, have the players count how many correct answers they have. The player with the most correct answers wins a prize.

Parlez-Vous Français?

Write some simple sentences on index cards, such as "Where is the bathroom?" "What time is it?" "What is your name?" "Where is the hotel?" and "Stop! Thief!" Using a French-English phrase book for travelers, write the French translations on separate cards. Place the French phrases facedown in a pile. Spread the English phrases faceup on the table so they're

all visible. Ask one player to pick a French card. She has thirty seconds to match it to the correct English phrase. If she's correct, she keeps the card. If she misses, she returns the card to the pile. Continue until all the cards are matched. Award a prize to the player with the most cards.

Prizes and Favors

- *Madeline* or other books in the series by Ludwig Bemelmans
- Posters of France
- French-English dictionaries
- Hair ribbons
- French music

Activities

Crêperie Chefs

Make crêpes before the party and refrigerate them. At the party, put out bowls of fresh berries, ice cream, chocolate sauce, chocolate spread, jam, whipped cream, and so on. Warm the crêpes in a pan or in the microwave and give one to each guest. Let them fill their crêpes with their favorite ingredients.

Madeline Hats

Have each guest cut a circle the size of a dinner plate from yellow poster board. Place a yellow paper bowl upside down on the middle of the circle. Trace the bowl and cut out a circle approximately an inch closer to the center from the bowl outline. Glue the bowl onto the poster board rim. Wrap a long blue ribbon around the hat and tie it in a bow. Let the ends hang down the back. Or let the guests decorate their hats with crepe paper, markers, glitter, and so on.

Refreshments

- Madeline's Hat Cake: Place a small bowl upside down on top of a round cake and frost both yellow. Tie blue ribbon around the bowl.
- Baguettes stuffed with ham and soft cheese
- French pastries
- Grape juice served in wineglasses

The Magic School Bus: In the Time of the Dinosaurs

When you hop aboard the Magic School Bus, you take a magical trip—to outer space, inside a hurricane, or to the bottom of the sea. Come along with your fun and wacky teacher, Ms. Frizzle, as we travel back to the age of dinosaurs!

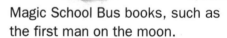

Invitation

Time Line

1. Draw a time line down the center of a long strip of paper.
2. Using colorful markers, mark the party date on one end of the time line. Include a breakdown of party events, such as "11:00—Board the Magic School Bus," "11:30—Travel Through Time for an Archaeological Dig," "12:00—Dig Dinosaur Eggs."
3. At the other end, mark the Triassic, Jurassic, and Cretaceous periods.
4. Between the party date and the prehistoric periods, include recent holidays, guests' birthdays, and historical dates mentioned in other

Magic School Bus books, such as the first man on the moon.

5. Roll the time line, secure it with a dinosaur sticker, and mail it in a tube decorated with dinosaur stickers.

Costumes

Have guests come dressed as scientists or archaeologists. Or suggest that they come dressed as Arnold (or a female counterpart). You or another adult could dress as Ms. Frizzle and wear a red wig and outrageous clothes featuring dinosaurs. Decorate the tops of your shoes with small plastic

dinosaur figurines and wear dinosaur earrings.

Decorations

- Drape green streamers from the ceiling to create vines.
- Tape trees and bushes made from green and brown construction paper to the walls. Or set out a variety of fake or real potted plants.
- Tape pictures of dinosaurs to the walls.
- Set out toy dinosaurs and large Styrofoam or plastic "dinosaur" eggs.

- Hang signs that label the different time periods and have the kids walk under the signs as they travel back to dinosaur time.
- Make a giant asteroid by filling a garbage bag with leaves or rags and then covering it with foil. Set it in one corner of the room.
- Set the table with a dinosaur-themed tablecloth and matching paper tableware.
- Create a nest centerpiece from excelsior (available at craft stores) or twigs and straw and fill the nest with big plastic eggs.

Games

Dino Identification

Hold up a picture of a dinosaur and choose someone to identify it. If he gets it right, award him a prize and have him sit out the rest of the game. If he misses, ask another player to identify it. Keep playing until everyone identifies a dinosaur and wins a prize. Or ask trivia questions about the dinosaurs and let the kids race to answer. The player with the most correct answers wins a prize.

Prizes & Favors

- *The Magic School Bus: In the Time of the Dinosaurs* or other books in the series by Joanna Cole
- Toy dinosaurs
- Dinosaur stickers
- Dinosaur books

Dinosaur Egg Hunt

Place a small dinosaur, some jelly-beans, or a sticker inside a large plastic egg, one for each player. Hide the eggs all over the yard or party room and have the kids hunt for them. When everyone has found an egg, have the kids open them to discover the surprises inside.

Activities

New Species

Provide the kids with paper or poster board. Give them markers and have them create a new dinosaur, such as a "Bananasaurus Rex," "Sockosaur," "Potosaur," or "Frizzeratops." Show the dinosaurs to the group when they're finished. Then have the kids each tell part of a story about the new dinosaurs.

Archaeology Kits

Have the kids glue pictures of their favorite dinosaurs onto shoeboxes or school supply boxes. Set out puffy paints, markers, stickers, and other supplies to decorate the boxes. Fill the boxes with archaeology supplies, such as small paintbrushes, tweezers, magnifying glasses, colored pencils, note pads, glue, and so on.

What Happened to the Dinosaurs?

Ask the kids to imagine why the dinosaurs disappeared. Give them paper, markers, paint, and so on and have them illustrate their reasons.

Refreshments

- Dinosaur eggs (dyed hard-boiled eggs)
- Dino-burgers (hamburgers)
- Edible plants (lettuce, celery, bean sprouts, fruits, and vegetables)
- Milk served in coconut shells
- Dinosaur Cake: Frost a sheet cake half green and half blue to make foliage and lakes. Add dinosaur fig-urines, tiny trees, and small candy eggs. Add a pile of chocolate frost-ing to make a volcano. Top it with red frosting.

Magic Tree House: Ghost Town at Sundown

You never know what's going to happen when you climb up to the Magic Tree House. Watch out for Wild West horses, cowboys, and even ghosts at our *Magic Tree House* party!

Invitation

Magic Tree House

1. Cut a tree trunk from brown construction paper. Cut a treetop from green construction paper.
2. Glue the treetop onto the trunk.
3. Cut 2 tree houses from brown construction paper. Make them a little smaller than the treetop.
4. Cut a door in one of the tree houses.
5. Leaving the door open, glue that tree house over the other.
6. On the outside of the door, write "I wish we could go there . . ."
7. On the inside of the door, write "Come to our Magic Tree House Party and be in a Ghost Town at Sundown!" Add the party details.
8. Close the door and seal it with a balloon sticker.
9. Place the invitation in a large manila envelope.
10. On the back of the envelope, write a riddle from the book, such as "Out of the blue, my lonely voice calls out to you. Who am I? Am I?" Or write your own riddle about the party.

Costumes

Encourage your guests to come dressed as characters from the book: Jack, Annie, Lonesome Luke, Slim

Cooley, Sunset, or Dusty. Or have them come dressed in Wild West clothes. Provide accessories, such as bandannas and lassos, when they arrive. You or another adult could dress as Morgan in long robes.

Decorations

- Cover the front door with a giant construction paper or cardboard cutout of the Magic Tree House. Hang a sign near it that reads "I wish we could go there . . ."

- Set cardboard or Styrofoam tombstones on the lawn. Write funny epitaphs or riddles on them.
- In the front hallway, hang a sign that reads "Welcome to Rattlesnake Flats." Hang signs over the doorways that name the various places in the ghost town, such as the hotel, saloon, and general store.
- Make ghosts from white poster board, decorate them with funny faces, and hang them from the ceiling with black string. Or hang white

cloths over helium balloons and float them to the ceiling.

- Tape pictures of horses to the walls and set out horse figurines.
- Tuck some rubber rattlesnakes into corners, in the furniture, and under the table to give the kids an occasional scare.
- Set out barrels, tumbleweeds, lassos, saddles, or other Wild West items.
- Set the table with a western-themed tablecloth or red bandanna-style tablecloth. Use canteens to serve beverages and tin plates to serve food.
- Play Old West piano music, such as "Red River Valley."

Games

Cowboy Boot Race

Divide the players into two teams. Give the first players a pair of thick socks and a pair of cowboy boots. At the word "Go!" the players must put on the socks and boots then race to the other side of the yard and back.

Prizes & Favors
- *Magic Tree House: Ghost Town at Sundown* or other books in the series by Mary Pope Osborne
- Cowboy hats
- Canteens
- Riddle books

When they return, they must remove the boots and socks and pass them to the next teammates in line. The first team to finish the race wins a prize.

Horse Ropin'

Back a large picture of a horse head with cardboard and attach it to a sawhorse. Loop rope into a large lasso. Let each player have three tries to encircle the horse head with the rope. Award prizes to players who lasso the horse.

Riddles

Read a riddle from a kids' riddle book. The player who guesses the correct answer wins a prize but sits out for the rest of the game. Repeat until everyone wins a prize.

Activities

Wild West Nicknames

Let the guests give one another Wild West nicknames or let them choose their own names. Offer suggestions if they need help, such as "Slim," "Marshal," "One Eye," "Baldy," "Toothless," and so on. Have the kids write their nicknames on adhesive nametags and wear them for the rest of the party. Have everyone call one another by their nicknames. For added fun, if someone calls a guest by her real name, he gets a point. The player with the fewest points wins a prize.

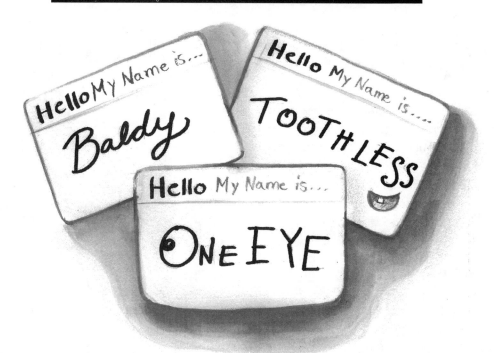

Cowboy Hats

Give each guest a cowboy hat. Let the kids decorate their hats with glitter glue, puffy paints, feathers, sequins, ribbon trim, jewels, permanent markers, decals, and so on.

Ghost Stories

Make an edible campfire—spread refried beans on a large platter and stick red and yellow triangular tortilla chips in the beans so they look like red-hot flames. Dim the lights and give the guests each a small flashlight. Gather the kids around the campfire and share ghost stories or read stories from favorite scary books. Let the kids eat the campfire when the ghost stories are done.

Refreshments

- Rattlesnakes in buns (hot dogs)
- Black coffee (hot chocolate)
- Sausage and egg biscuits
- Trail mix
- Tree House Cake: Frost a square cake with chocolate frosting and add tree house details. Write "I wish we could go there . . ." at the top.

My Father's Dragon

We're off to Wild Island to save a captive dragon. Won't you come along and help? Of course, there are those crocodiles in the way . . . but we've packed a bag of party tricks to get us through the dangers!

Invitation

Knapsack

1. Fold brown construction paper in half.
2. Draw a knapsack so the top of the sack is on the fold.
3. Cut out the knapsack, leaving the fold intact.
4. Draw a crocodile on the outside of the knapsack and write "Come to Wild Island . . ." below it.
5. On the inside, draw a dragon and write ". . . And Help Us Save My Father's Dragon!" and the party details below it.
6. Draw a dragon on the front of the envelope and a crocodile on the back.

Costumes

Ask the kids to come dressed as characters from the book. Or when they arrive, pass out costume accessories

to represent the animals mentioned in the book, such as fangs for a crocodile, a fake-fur tail for a monkey, a striped shirt for a tiger, wings for a dragon, and so on.

Decorations

- Cover the walls with green crepe paper.
- Tape palm, mahogany, and banyan trees made from construction paper to the walls.
- Drape green streamers from the ceiling to create vines.

- Spread blue fabric across the middle of the room to make a river.
- Copy the maps of Tangerina and Wild Island. Tape the maps to the walls. Add details, such as bodies of water, rivers, wild animals, and so on. Or let the kids add the details during activity time.
- Tape a huge construction paper dragon to a wall.
- Tape pictures of wild animals and sea life to the walls. Don't forget the crocodiles!
- Put up signposts directing the guests to various places on Wild Island, such as "Ocean Rocks," "Clearings," "Dragon's Ferry," and "Beginning of River." Add signs that read "Beware of Crocodile!" "Do Not Feed the Animals!" and "To summon dragon, yank the crank."

Games

Knapsack Relay
Pack two complete adult-size outfits (pants, shirt, socks, shoes, hat, gloves, belt, and scarf) into two knapsacks. Divide the players into two teams and have each team stand on

one side of the "river." At the word "Go!" the first players must open their knapsacks, put on the outfits, and jump across the river with the knapsacks. Once on the other side, they must remove the outfits, pack them into the knapsacks, and jump back over the river with the knapsacks. The next teammates in line repeat the tasks. Award a prize to the first team to finish the relay.

Cargo Relay

Divide the players into two teams and give each team a sleeping bag. The first players must crawl into their teams' sleeping bags. The next teammates in line must drag the sleeping bags through the "swamp" to the other side of the room. The teammates then switch places, with the first players dragging their teammates in the bags back to their teams. Two more teammates repeat the tasks. The first team that finishes the relay wins a prize.

Prizes & Favors
- *My Father's Dragon* or other books in the series by Ruth Stiles Gannett
- Bubble gum in wild flavors
- Compasses
- Colorful combs, hairbrushes, and hair accessories

Ocean Rocks Walk

Tear the edges of several sheets of black construction paper to look like jagged rocks. Place the rocks four to five feet apart in a circle. Tell the players water surrounds the rocks and crocodiles are in the water. At the word "Go!" players leap from rock to rock around the circle. If a player falls in the water, she must start over. Time each player and award a prize to the fastest leaper.

Activities

Map Making

Give the kids large sheets of white paper and markers. Have them draw Wild Island. Or have them draw maps from the party house to their own houses to see if the others can figure out where they live.

Dragons

Give the guests each one clean sock. Set out decorating supplies, such as felt, sequins, glitter, permanent markers, puffy paints, appliques, and googly eyes, along with glue and scissors. Have the kids make dragon puppets. Put on a puppet show, videotape the performance, and show the videotape during the party.

Magnified Mystery

Have the guests each look at something in the room or yard with a magnifying glass. Have them draw exactly what they see. Show each drawing and see if the other kids can identify the magnified objects.

Refreshments

- Peanut-butter-and-jelly sandwiches
- Apples, tangerines, and cranberries
- Apple, tangerine, and cranberry juices
- Lollipops and gum
- Lollipop Cake: Frost a round cake with pink frosting and add a long strip of licorice to make the stick. Insert lollipops all over the cake.

Peter Pan

We're headed to Neverland for a *Peter Pan* party! Sprinkle on some fairy dust and you'll find yourself flying through the air! But beware—there are dangers ahead. Tick . . . tock . . . tick . . . tock . . .

Invitation

Neverland Map

1. Fold white construction paper in half.
2. On the outside, draw a map of Neverland. Label the Lost Boys' home, the mermaids' lagoon, Marooner's Rock, Hook's ship, Tiger Lily's home, and Croc's lagoon.
3. Add an X to mark the guest's home and an X in the middle of Neverland to mark the party home. Draw a wavy line that connects the Xs.
4. Write the party details inside.
5. Pour a little glitter along the fold of the card before you insert it into the envelope.
6. Use "Neverland" as the return address. Print "Watch out for fairy dust!" on the back.

Costumes

Ask guests to come dressed as characters from the book: Peter, Wendy, John, Michael, Hook, Tinker Bell, a Lost Boy, pirate, member of the Piccaninny tribe, or Croc. Or turn the guests into pirates when they arrive by supplying eye patches, big-buckled belts, bandannas, and stuffed parrots.

Decorations

- Have the kids enter the party room through a large box painted like a hollow tree. Decorate the box with construction paper leaves. Label it the "Never Tree."
- Set out small, gray-painted boxes that are strong enough for the kids to sit on. Cover the box tops with large gray poster board circles to make the boxes look like mushrooms.

- Tape trees made from brown and green construction paper to the walls.
- Hang green streamers from the ceiling to create vines.
- Spread blue fabric on the floor for the crocodile lagoon. Make Croc's head out of a box. Tape the box closed. Draw a zigzag across the middle of three sides of the box. Using a utility knife, cut along the line to form Croc's teeth. Cut a straight line through the middle of

the fourth side, splitting the box into two pieces. Place the top piece on the bottom piece, tilting it so it looks like an open mouth. Secure the angle with duct tape. Paint the crocodile's face and then set a ticking clock inside. Put Croc's head in the lagoon so it looks as if he's submerged in the water.

Prizes and Favors
- *Peter Pan* by J. M. Barrie
- Fairy dust (body glitter)
- Bells
- Kites
- Pan pipes

- Tape a picture of Hook's ship to the wall behind the lagoon. Or make the ship out of a large box, hoist a flag, and let the kids climb aboard.

Games

Walk the Plank
Lay a brick on each side of the lagoon. Set a six-foot-long two-by-four on top of the bricks. Make sure the bricks are level and the board isn't wobbly. Have the kids take turns "walking the plank." If a player makes it all the way across without falling into the water, he wins a prize. If he falls into the

lagoon, he must try again until he makes it across.

Tick . . . Tock . . .

Set a timer for three minutes and hide it somewhere in the room. Tell the kids they have to find the ticking crocodile before he attacks. The first player to find Croc wins a prize and gets to hide the ticking crocodile for the rest of the group.

Activities

Swashbuckler Swords

Cut swords from cardboard or poster board. Round the tips for safety. Let the kids decorate their swords with gold, silver, and black paint as well as with markers, glitter, stickers, and so on.

Pirate Songs

Sing pirate songs, such as "Yo, ho, ho, the frisky plank, you walks along it so, till it goes down and you goes down to Davy Jones below!" (Use the tune for "Jingle Bells" or make up your own tune.) Make up your own pirate songs, too.

Refreshments

- Pirate's Punch: Mix tropical fruit juices together and serve the punch in scooped-out coconuts with crazy straws.
- Walk-the-Planks (celery sticks filled with peanut butter and dotted with raisins)
- Serve meat stew and call it "crocodile stew."
- Fairy dust (Pixy Sticks)

Pippi Longstocking

Pippi Longstocking is an amazing, creative, imaginative, and remarkable girl. Can you imagine going to one of Pippi's parties? It only takes a little of Pippi's imagination to have a lot of fun!

Invitation

Pippi's Longstocking

1. Cut a long sock from white construction paper or poster board.
2. Add red stripes.
3. Write the party details on the white spaces between the red stripes.
4. Or buy long white socks and add stripes with red permanent marker.
5. Write the party details on the white sections of the sock.
6. Use "Villa Villekula" as the return address.

Costumes

Ask guests to come dressed as Pippi Longstocking or as other characters from the book. Or dot eyebrow-penciled freckles all over the guests' faces and give them long stockings when they arrive. The stockings can be red-and-white striped, one black and one brown, or any color at all. They don't have to match—Pippi's didn't! Braid the girls' hair into pigtails.

Decorations

- Fill the party room with unusual knickknacks and mismatched furniture (borrowed from friends). Throw colorful blankets over the sofas and chairs.
- Put out lots of flowers to simulate Pippi's overgrown garden.
- Display nautical items, such as fishnets, ship flags, pirate clothes, plastic fish, and so on.
- Dress a stuffed monkey in blue pants, yellow shirt, and white straw

hat. Name him Mr. Nilsson and use him as a centerpiece.

• Place balloons around the party room. Hang colorful streamers from the ceiling.

Games

Pancake Flipping Contest

Divide the players into pairs. Give one player in each pair a spatula and a stack of ten cooled pancakes. Give her partner a pan or large plate. Stand the partners a few feet apart. Have the player with the pancakes turn her back to her partner and flip the pancakes (one at a time) over her shoulder with the spatula while her partner tries to catch them. Award a point for each pancake he catches. Give each pair a turn to flip pancakes. The pair with the most points wins a prize.

Egg Toss

If you aren't brave enough to toss raw eggs like Pippi, substitute them with hard-boiled eggs or water balloons. In any case, play this game outside! Pair

up players and have them stand about three feet from their partners. Give an egg to one player in each pair. At the word "Go!" he must toss the egg to his partner. If she drops the egg, the pair is out of the game. After all the

eggs have been tossed once, those pairs left in the game must take a step back from each other and then toss again. Repeat the process until there's only one pair left. Award them a prize.

Prizes and Favors

- *Pippi Longstocking* or other books in the series by Astrid Lindgren
- Books on Sweden
- Music boxes
- Decorative pins
- Toy monkeys

Thing-Finders

Make a list of several things around the house, yard, or neighborhood. Anything will do, but the more unusual the item, the better. Divide the players into two teams and give each team a copy of the list. Give the teams thirty minutes to find as many things on the list as they can. (Be sure to set search boundaries.) The team that finds the most things wins a prize.

Activities

Dance the Schottische

Turn on polka music. Teach the kids how to polka or let them make up their own dances.

Old Sea Chest

Put a number of interesting items in a big chest or in a box painted to look like an old sea chest. You might include a felt scrap, boot, toilet paper tube, eggbeater, boxer shorts, stuffed monkey, large seashell, colored rock, or ugly necklace. Have the guests each pull out something from the chest. Give them one minute to think of something funny to do with their items. Have them take turns doing skits with their items.

Seashell Scenes

Give guests stiff white paper and a variety of seashells. Let them create collages using the shells and craft supplies, such as glue, glitter, jewels, markers, paint, and so on.

Refreshments

- Pancakes—but not the ones from the game!
- Scrambled eggs—but not the ones from the egg toss!
- Sausage and ham
- Meatball and ham sandwiches
- Pineapple pudding
- Swedish cookies and buns
- Decaffeinated mochas or hot cocoa with whipped cream

Robin Hood

Gather your Merry Boys and Girls and head for Sherwood Forest, where you're apt to meet all kinds of interesting people. Keep your bows and arrows handy for games of skill against the evil Sheriff of Nottingham!

Invitation

Cap Filled with Gold

1. Make a template of the side of a pointed hat like the one Robin Hood wore.
2. Use the template to cut 2 hats from green felt or construction paper.
3. Glue the hats together, leaving the bottom open.
4. Write the party details on parchment paper. Roll it, secure it with a gold sticker, and place it inside the hat along with some gold coins.
5. Glue a feather onto the side of the hat.
6. Use "Sherwood Forest" as the return address.

Costumes

Ask the guests to come dressed as characters from the book: Robin Hood, Friar Tuck, King Richard, Maid Marion, Sheriff of Nottingham, or Little John.

When the guests arrive, provide them with costume accessories, such as toy bows and suction-cup arrows, feathered caps, and cloaks.

Decorations

• It's easiest to create Sherwood Forest in your back yard. But if you want to host the party inside, cover the walls with giant trees made from brown and green construction or crepe paper.

• Paint a large box gray and cut out an opening to make a cave.

• Spread blue fabric on the floor to make a river. Make a bridge over the river by setting a wooden plank on bricks.

• Hang green streamers from the ceiling to create vines.

• Have pictures of animals, such as deer, wolves, and wild pigs, peeking out from behind the trees.

• Cover the table with brown paper to make it look like a fallen tree. Pile chocolate gold coins on the table and label the heap "The King's Ransom."

• Use a small chest filled with coins and candy jewelry as a centerpiece.

Games

Bull's-Eye

Set up a target in the yard. Let the Merry Boys and Girls take turns trying to shoot the suction-cup toy arrows into the bull's-eye. Be sure to supervise the game and make sure no one

is in the arrows' path during play. Award a point for every bull's-eye shot. The archer with the most points wins a prize.

Rob from the Rich

Tape a gold coin to the back of each player's shirt. Tell the players that for the next thirty minutes, they're to steal the gold coins from one another without getting caught. If a player catches someone stealing her coin,

Prizes and Favors
- *Robin Hood*
- Coin purses or pouches
- Archery books
- Toy horns

the thief must return the stolen coin and forfeit his own coin to her. During the half-hour, play another game or do an activity. When time is up, the player with the most coins wins a prize.

Activities

Robin Hood's Cap

Make a template of the side of a pointed hat like the one Robin Hood wore. Make the hat large enough to fit a guest's head. Have the guests each use the template to cut two hats from green felt or construction paper. Staple the hats together, leaving the bottom open. Provide feathers, glitter, puffy paint, and so on for the kids to decorate their hats.

Swords and Daggers

Cut swords and daggers from cardboard. Round the edges for safety. Let the kids decorate them with poster paint, markers, glitter, sequins, jewels, stickers, and other supplies.

Merry Boys and Girls Goblets

Have the kids decorate plastic goblets with puffy paints, stickers, jewels, glitter, and permanent markers. During the meal, fill the goblets with grog (sparkling soda and fruit juice) and have the guests each make a toast.

Refreshments

- Chocolate gold coins
- Barbecued wild pig legs (chicken legs) and deer jerky (beef jerky)
- Forest mix (roasted nuts, dried fruit, and seeds)
- Log cake with chocolate frosting

Winnie-the-Pooh

Let's have an exciting party with Pooh and the 100 Aker Wood gang. We'll have an absoposilutely bouncy, trouncy, flouncy, pouncy good time!

Invitation

Pooh's Blue Balloon

1. Cut out a picture of Winnie-the-Pooh and back it with cardboard.
2. Write the party details on paper and glue it onto the back of Pooh.
3. Blow up a blue balloon.
4. Make it look as if Pooh is holding onto the balloon by tying one end of ribbon to the balloon and the other end to a small hole in Pooh's paw.
5. Hand-deliver the invitation. Or leave the balloon deflated and mail the invitation.

Costumes

Invite the guests to come dressed as characters from the book: Pooh, Piglet, Eeyore, Tigger, Rabbit, Kanga, or Roo. When the guests arrive, accessorize the costumes with face paints, ears made from stiff felt or craft foam attached to headbands, rope tails, and so on.

Decorations

- Tape trees made from brown and green construction paper to the walls.
- Hang brown and green streamers from the ceiling to create vines and tree branches.
- Create big boulders by painting boxes gray.

- Display stuffed animals of Pooh and his pals.
- Make the table look like a tree stump by covering it with a brown paper tablecloth. Cut leaf-shaped place mats from green construction paper. Use a stuffed Pooh and a big jar of honey as a centerpiece.
- Hang signs like those in the book: "North Pole—Discovered by Pooh—

Pooh Found It," "Ples Ring If An Rnser Is Reqird," "Pooh's Corner," and "It's Me Piglet, Help Help."

Games

Poohball

Tape the top and bottom of a large box shut. Cut a semicircle at the bottom of each of two opposite sides to make a tunnel. Paint the box to look like a wooden bridge. Lay blue paper on the floor through the tunnel to make it look like a river running under the bridge. Wrap prizes, one for each guest, and place them on the paper a few feet from one of the box's openings. Ask the players trivia questions about Pooh. The first player to answer a question correctly gets a tennis ball. Have the player stand five feet away from the box's other opening and roll the ball under the bridge. If the ball hits a prize, he gets to keep it. If not, he doesn't get another chance until all the other players have had a turn. Keep playing until each player wins a prize.

Tigger's Whoop-de-Dooper Bouncing Games

Balloon Bounce: See how long the players can bounce balloons in the air. The player who lasts the longest wins a prize. Ball Bounce: Buy rubber balls for all the guests and let them bounce the balls against a wall as many times in a row as they can. The player with

Prizes and Favors

- *Winnie-the-Pooh* or other books in the series by A. A. Milne
- Pooh's special pencil case filled with colored pencils, erasers, rulers, and other art supplies
- Pooh paraphernalia
- Blue balloons

the most bounces wins a prize. Circle Bounce: Have the kids form a circle and give each player a ball. Every time you say "Bounce!" they must bounce their balls to the right. If a player doesn't catch the ball, he's out of the game. When there's only one player left, award her a prize.

Eeyore's Tail

Make Eeyore tails from gray felt. Cut fringe at the end of the tails. Stick a tail onto the back of each player's shirt with double-sided tape. When you call out "Eeyore!" have the kids run around and grab as many tails as they can within one minute. The player who collects the most tails wins a prize.

Activities

What's a Heffalump?

Draw seven parallel lines on white paper, making eight sections. Make a photocopy of it for each guest. Give the kids pens, pencils, and markers, and ask them to draw the top of the Heffalump's head and eyebrows in the first sections. When they're finished, ask each to fold the paper along the first line so the top section doesn't show. Have them pass their papers to the right. Tell them not to look at the folded sections. Ask them to draw the Heffalump's ears in the second sections. Repeat for the eyes, nose, mouth and chin, body and arms, legs, and

feet. When the Heffalumps are complete, open the papers and take a look!

Pooh Comic Strips

Using inexpensive picture books, cut out several pictures of Pooh, Piglet, and the rest of the gang. Cut out several props as well, such as the honey pot, tree, kite, and so on. Give the guests white construction paper, glue, and markers. Let the kids take turns choosing characters or props until all the cutouts are chosen. Have the guests use their cutouts to create Pooh comic strips. When the guests finish their Pooh comic strips, have each guest show and read hers to the group.

Refreshments

- Hot biscuits or popovers served with honey
- Peanut-butter-and-honey sandwiches
- Honey-flavored cereals
- 100 Aker Woods mix (cereals, seeds, raisins, and chopped nuts)
- Make "Tigger milk" by serving chocolate milk with orange or yellow candy swizzle sticks.

The Wonderful Wizard of Oz

We're off to see the Wizard because he's hosting a big party for Dorothy, the Cowardly Lion, the Scarecrow, the Tin Woodman, and us! Just click your heels three times and follow the Yellow Brick Road. You'll soon be in Oz!

Invitation

Yellow Brick Road

1. Accordion-fold a large sheet of yellow construction paper 3 times, dividing the paper into 4 sections.
2. Cut out a wide, curvy "road" from one fold to the other.
3. On the first folded section, write "Follow the Yellow Brick Road."
4. Unfold the paper and write the party details along the road.
5. At the end of the road, glue on a green faux jewel and write "Oz" below it.
6. Use "Oz" as the return address.

Costumes

Ask your guests to come dressed as Dorothy, Toto, the Tin Woodman, the Cowardly Lion, the Scarecrow, Glinda the Good Witch, the Wicked Witch, the

Wizard of Oz, or a Munchkin. Provide face paints so the guests can accessorize their costumes when they arrive.

Decorations

- Float green balloons to the ceiling and cover the ceiling and walls with green crepe paper.
- Cover the table with a green tablecloth and use green tableware.
- Use green light bulbs and hang strings of green lights.
- Cover the furniture with green fabric.

- On the walls, hang murals of different places in the book: Dorothy's house in Kansas, the Yellow Brick Road going off into a poppy field, Munchkin Land, and the scary forest where the Wicked Witch lives.
- Set out bouquets of paper poppies.

Games

Colorful Sayings

Have the players sit in a circle and give each one a piece of paper in a different color. The first player must come up with a phrase that includes the color she has been given. For example, if she has blue, she might say, "I have the blues." The next player must come up with a phrase using his color. If a player cannot come up with a colorful phrase within fifteen seconds, she's out of the game. Continue until only one player remains and award him a prize.

"I'm Melting!"

Divide the players into two teams and have each team line up outside. Place

a kiddie pool of hot (but not scalding) water at the beginning of each line and place an ice cube at the end of each line. Give the players closest to the pools each a plastic cup. These players must fill their cups with water, and the cups are passed down the lines until they reach the last players. These players must pour what's left in the cups over the ice cubes. The cups are then passed back to the first players and the task is repeated. The first team to completely melt its ice cube wins a prize.

Prizes and Favors

- *The Wonderful Wizard of Oz* or other books in the series by L. Frank Baum
- Toy dogs or monkeys
- Magic wands from Glinda the Good Witch
- Bouquets of poppies or packets of poppy seeds

Activities

Pressed Poppy Bookmarks

Give each guest a heavy book, a piece of wax paper, and a California poppy (or any other small yellow flower). Have the kids fold their wax paper and set their flowers between the folds. Then have them carefully set their flowers between the pages of their books. While the flowers are being pressed, give each guest two bookmark-size strips of clear contact paper. Have the guests each peel off the protective back of one strip. Provide glitter, sequins, stickers, and other items to press onto the sticky side of the strip. Have each guest remove his flower from the book and press it onto the center of the strip. Remove the backs from the second strips and press them onto the first strips, sticky sides together. Finally, have the kids round the edges of their bookmarks and trim off any extra contact paper.

Oz Eyes

Draw the outline of a pair of 3-D glasses on poster board. Make an outline for each guest. Let the kids decorate their glasses with glitter, sequins, jewels, stickers, and so on. Have the kids cut out their glasses. Encourage them to be creative and cut wings, spikes, and other designs along the top of the frames. Lay the glasses flat, decorated-side down. Cut circles from green cellophane, making them slightly larger than the glasses' eyeholes. Glue the cellophane onto the glasses. Fold the glasses so they fit on the kids' faces.

Refreshments

- Sandwiches made with green bread (You can add green food coloring to homemade bread dough or ask a bakery to make green-tinted bread for you.)
- Green pudding
- Green cake frosted green (Tint white cake batter and frosting green with food coloring.)
- Green mint ice cream

The Adventures of Tom Sawyer

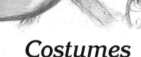

Tom Sawyer's adventures with Becky Thatcher, Huck Finn, and the gang make wonderful ideas for a party. Spend an evening at McDougal's Cave, look for pirate treasure, do a little whitewashing, and challenge a few superstitions. But watch out for that old dead cat at midnight!

Invitation

Whitewashed Picket Fence

1. Cut a large picket fence from white construction paper.
2. Write the party details on it with a white crayon.
3. Accordion-fold the fence and write "Come to Tom Sawyer's Party" on the top fold.
4. Place the invitation in a large envelope along with a watercolor paintbrush and a cake of watercolor paint.
5. On the back of the envelope, explain that the guest must paint the fence to find out about the party.

Costumes

Invite guests to come dressed as characters from the book, such as Tom, Becky, Huck Finn, or even Aunt Polly or Cousin Sid. When they arrive, offer them costume accessories, such as bandannas, straw hats, corncob pipes, suspenders, aprons, and so on.

Decorations

• Flatten several large boxes. In the middle of the party room, assemble the cardboard to make McDougal's Cave, using duct tape to hold it together. Paint the cave brown on

the outside. Hang polyester cob-webs, plastic spiders, and rubber bats from the cave's ceiling. Be sure to set rubber snakes on the cave's floor and a stuffed cat near its entrance. Give the kids flash-lights before they enter the cave.

- Along one wall of the party room, hang a white picket fence made from construction paper. Write slo-gans on it, such as "Tom loves Becky," "Huck Finn was here," and "Watch out for Aunt Polly!"

- In one corner, create a graveyard complete with cardboard tombstones painted gray. Write a creative epitaph on each one for each guest, such as

"Here lies Geoffie, laid to rest. Tried to cheat on his math test!"

Games

Fence-Painting Race

Divide the players into two teams and head for the nearest fence. Give each team a big paintbrush and a bucket of water. Place the two teams at oppo-site ends of the fence and mark a fin-ish line at the middle of the fence. At the word "Go!" the first players must "paint" their first slats with water. As soon as they're done, they must pass the brushes to the next teammates in line so they can paint the next slats.

Excitement builds as the teams paint closer and closer to each other! Award a prize to the first team that paints the final slat.

Slate Pictures

On index cards, write actions, such as eating pizza, getting your hair cut, taking a test, and so on. Set the cards facedown in a pile. Have the first player pick a card and draw the action with chalk on a large blackboard. (Or make a blackboard from black construction paper.) The first player to identify the action wins a point. Keep playing until everyone has had a turn to draw. The player with the most points wins a prize.

Sawyer's Superstitions

Write several superstitions on separate index cards. Find some in the book, such as "You can get rid of warts with spunk-water." Take others from everyday language, such as "If you make a face and the wind changes, your face will stay that way." Also write several real facts that sound like superstitions, such as "Milk makes your bones strong." Set the cards facedown in a pile. Have one player choose a card and read it out loud. Have him guess whether the sentence is a superstition or a fact. If he guesses correctly, he gets a prize. If not, he gets a ribbon. Continue until everyone has had a turn to draw a card. For added fun, have the kids make up superstitions and play again.

Snail Race

Collect snails from the yard. Draw a starting line and finish line on a sidewalk. Set the snails about six inches apart on the starting line and release them. Have the players choose their snails and watch them closely. The first snail to cross the finish line (or even get close to it) wins its owner a prize. Return the snails to the yard. You may want to substitute snails with frogs, turtles, or any critters of your choice.

Prizes and Favors
- *The Adventures of Tom Sawyer* by Mark Twain
- Paintbrushes and watercolors
- Marbles
- Gum
- Chocolate gold coins
- Colored chalk
- Kites

Activities

Tom's Whatnots and Thingamajigs

In separate paper bags, place items mentioned in the book, such as an apple, kite, rubber rat on a string, marbles, and so on. Give a bag to each guest. Have them look inside their bags and think of something

Eating a pizza

unusual to do with the items. Have each guest remove his item and tell how he would use it. For example, if he had an apple, he might use it as a paperweight.

Tom's Treasure

Wrap prizes in gold paper, one for each guest. Place the prizes in a small box spray-painted gold. Hide the gold box somewhere in the house or yard. Write clues, such as "Find the first clue under a shoe," that lead the kids around the house and yard until they finally reach the hidden treasure. Have them open the treasure and each take a prize.

Refreshments

- Picnic foods, such as ham sandwiches, chips, cookies, and lemonade
- Whitewashed Cake: Top a white-frosted cake with a small white plastic fence.
- Apples
- Doughnuts
- Bacon and eggs
- Fish sticks and corn on the cob

Anne of Green Gables

Everyone loves the imagination, creativity, and spunk of Anne of Green Gables. We're off to Prince Edward Island for a lovely party with Anne!

Invitation

Welcome to Avonlea!

1. Pick up a brochure on Prince Edward Island, Canada, at a local travel agency. Or photocopy a picture of the island.
2. Write the party details on white paper and attach it to the brochure. Or write party details on the back of the picture. In either case, welcome your guests to Avonlea and Green Gables.
3. Mail the invitation in a green envelope.

Costumes

Have your guests come dressed in their fanciest clothes (including a hat) for Anne's tea party. Suggest that they put flowers in their hair. Add eyebrow-penciled freckles to their faces when they arrive.

Decorations

- Hang a sign on the door welcoming the guests to Avonlea and Green Gables.
- Hang signs marking other places in the novel. Include the White Way of Delight, Lovers' Lane, Violet Vale, the Lake of Shining Waters, the Haunted Wood, and so on.
- Set out potted geraniums and write "Bonnie" on the pots. Fill vases with flowers.

• Cover the table with a white lace tablecloth and use an arrangement of roses and ferns as a centerpiece. Set the table with china and silver place settings.

Games

Avonlea Trivia

Write a list of questions that relate to the book, such as "What are the names of Anne's adoptive parents?" "Who is Anne's bosom friend?" "What happened when Anne invited Diana to a tea party?" "Who called Anne 'carrots' at school?" and so on. Give each player a pencil and paper. Read each question out loud and have the players write down their answers. Award a point for each correct answer. The player with the most points wins a prize.

Poetry Mix-Up

Write or type some famous poems onto separate sheets of paper. Count the lines or stanzas and then cut the poems in half, dividing them into

"beginnings" and "endings." Give one half to each player. Give the kids two minutes to match beginnings and endings. When time is up, have the players read their complete poems. (This may be funny if the halves aren't matched correctly!) Award prizes to the pairs who correctly matched their halves.

Prizes and Favors
- *Anne of Green Gables* or other books in the series by L. M. Montgomery
- Bookmarks
- Flower corsages
- Teacups
- Poetry books

Activities

The Lady of Shallot
Have the kids act out "The Lady of Shallot" by Alfred, Lord Tennyson. Provide costumes for the characters, such as long dresses, gloves, scarves, hats, and jewelry. Have the kids use props, such as a blue fabric river, boxes painted gray for the towers of Camelot, and a large box for a boat. Read the poem out loud as the kids pantomime each line. Have them take turns acting out different parts. Videotape the performance and show the videotape during the party.

High Tea

Host a tea party complete with herbal tea, fancy outfits, and a table set with a linen tablecloth, your best china, and silver place settings. Serve finger sandwiches and cookies with the tea. For added fun, make your favorite taffy recipe and have the kids pull the taffy before the tea.

Flower Wreaths

Provide real or fake flowers with long flexible stems. Have the guests weave and tie the flower stems together to make wreaths for their hair.

Refreshments

- Cold tongue (This should provide some squeals! You'll find it at a deli or gourmet grocery store. Ask the butcher for serving suggestions.)
- Lemon or cherry pies with whipped cream
- Fresh bread or biscuits with plum or crabapple preserves
- Brown-sugar cookies
- Fruitcake and layer cake
- Ice cream

Bunnicula: A Rabbit-Tale of Mystery

What's all the fuss about a sweet little rabbit named Bunnicula? Uncover the truth about the vampire bunny living with Toby and Pete Monroe at a *Bunnicula* party!

Invitation

Vampire Bunny

1. Draw a picture of a cute bunny on construction paper.
2. Cut it out and add construction paper vampire fangs made to fit the bunny's mouth.
3. Fold black construction paper in half.
4. Glue Bunnicula inside.
5. Cut slits in the front of the card so it looks like a cage door. Make the bars wide enough to hide Bunnicula's fangs when the card is closed.
6. Write the party details in white ink below Bunnicula.

Costumes

Ask the kids to come dressed as bunnies. Or when they arrive, provide them with bunny accessories, such as tails made from cotton ball clusters,

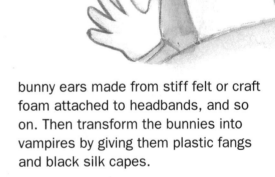

bunny ears made from stiff felt or craft foam attached to headbands, and so on. Then transform the bunnies into vampires by giving them plastic fangs and black silk capes.

Decorations

- Make a bunny cage out of a large box. Cut out a door on one side and then cut vertical bars in it to make it look like a cage door. Paint the box black and write "Bunnicula" on the front.
- Set out toy rabbits.

- Use a stuffed cat and dog to be Harold and Chester. Wrap a collar with a nametag around each animal's neck.
- Tape posters of scary movies like *Dracula* to the walls.
- Dim the lights and cover the walls and windows with black crepe paper for a scary effect.
- Use carrots as the centerpiece.
- Make poster board vampire fangs for place cards and construction paper bunny faces for place mats.
- Play creepy music.

Games

Bunnicula's Vampire Hunt

Choose one player to leave the room. Have another player hide a stuffed bunny or a picture of a bunny somewhere in the party room. Ask the first player to return. Tell her she must find Bunnicula before he turns into a vampire. Set a timer for two minutes. If the player finds Bunnicula before the timer goes off, she wins a prize and gets to hide the bunny for the next player. But if the timer goes off before she finds Bunnicula, both the bunny

and the player turn into vampires. Using a washable red marker, mark two dots on the player's neck. She doesn't get a prize, but she gets to hide the bunny for the next player.

What Tastes White?

Collect several white foods, such as mashed potatoes, plain yogurt, oatmeal, cauliflower, white frosting, a vanilla milkshake, vanilla ice cream, tofu, cream cheese, and so on. Seat the players at the table and give each one a pencil, paper, paper plate, spoon, and blindfold. After the players blindfold themselves, spoon a small amount of the first white food onto their plates. They must taste the food and write down what they think it is— while still blindfolded! When the players have tasted all the food, have them remove their blindfolds and read their answers (if they're legible!). Award a prize to the player who correctly identifies the most food.

Prizes and Favors
- *Bunnicula* or other books in the series by James Howe
- Toy rabbits
- Vampire books
- Rabbit books

Activities

Bunny Cupcakes

Make cupcakes and let the kids decorate them to look like bunnies, using frosting, decorative candies, licorice, marshmallows, and so on.

Sock Bunniculas

Give each guest a white sock. Have the kids stuff their socks with polyester filling. Wrap a rubber band around the middle of each sock to form Bunnicula's head and body. Let the kids detail their Bunniculas using permanent markers and puffy paints. Provide other decorating supplies, such as cotton balls, pompoms, googly eyes, ribbon, and floppy ears made from felt.

Refreshments

- Carrots
- Veggies and dips, including garlic dip
- White foods
- Cheese and crackers
- Vegetable juice
- Milk served in pet dishes

Charlie and the Chocolate Factory

Follow Charlie into the magical world of candy as we take a trip to Willy Wonka's Chocolate Factory. You'll have a sweet time with all the goodies to come!

Invitation

Candy Wrapper

1. Cut a ticket from gold foil.
2. With a marker, write "Charlie's Chocolate Factory Party" on one side of the ticket and the party details on the other.
3. Carefully unwrap a candy bar.
4. Slip the ticket into the candy bar wrapper and tape the wrapper closed.
5. Write "Open me!" on the outside.
6. Use "Willy Wonka's Chocolate Factory" as the return address.

Costumes

Ask your guests to come dressed as characters from the book or as their favorite candy. Choose one guest to be Willy Wonka and provide a black top hat, plum-colored coat, green trousers, and gray gloves when he arrives.

Decorations

- Make the Chocolate Room by covering the walls with brown crepe paper.
- Place candy bars around the room.
- Make a candy bar tree from brown and green construction paper. Tape the tree to the wall and tape small candies like Hershey's Kisses to the leaves.
- Spell "Welcome to the Chocolate Factory" with wrapped candies glued onto poster board. Tape the sign to the front door.

- Make the Pink Boat by painting a large box pink and gluing candies onto it. Put it in the middle of the room.
- Turn another room into the Inventing Room by displaying cooking utensils, baking ingredients, and candies.

Games

Chocolate Puzzles

Carefully cut a chocolate bar into small pieces. Place the pieces in a bowl. Repeat so each player has a bowl with the same number of choco- late pieces. At the word "Go!" the players must put together their chocolate bars. The first player to finish the puzzle wins a prize. When everyone finishes, let the kids eat their chocolate puzzles.

Candy Bar Taste Test

Break a variety of candy bars into pieces and place each bar's pieces in a separate bowl. Give the players pencil and paper. Pass around the first bowl and have the players each taste a piece. Have them write down their guesses of the candy bar's name.

Repeat until the players have tested a piece from each bowl. Read the correct candy bar names and award a prize to the player who correctly identifies the most candy bars.

Prizes and Favors
- *Charlie and the Chocolate Factory* or *Charlie and the Great Glass Elevator* by Roald Dahl
- Giant candy bars
- Canes made of wooden dowels with gold-sprayed tips
- Candy necklaces

Candy Costs
Set a variety of candies on the table. Write down the cost of each candy. Give the kids pencils and paper. Each player must write down how much she thinks each candy costs. After all the players have guessed, read the correct costs. The player who guesses the most correct costs gets first choice of the candies on the table. Let the second-place winner have second choice of the candies, and so on until all the candies are taken. (Make sure you have as many kinds of candy as there are guests!)

Activities

Chocolate Factories

Give each guest a shoebox. Provide craft supplies such as construction and crepe paper, glitter, poster paints, markers, glue, scissors, string, and so on. Set out bowls of wrapped candies. Have the kids create their own chocolate factories using their imaginations and the supplies you provided. When they're finished, let them give one another chocolate factory tours.

Chocolate Grab Bags

Set out several varieties of chocolate candies and bars. Give the guests sandwich bags and let them take turns choosing items to take home. Tie the bags with ribbons.

Refreshments

- Be sure to balance the candy intake with healthy foods, such as sandwiches, fruit and veggies, and soup.
- Hot chocolate
- Fudge

Charlotte's Web

Let's join Charlotte, Wilbur, Fern, and Avery at the local county fair! There are games, rides, prizes, and good old country fair food! Join in some TERRIFIC —make that RADIANT—fun!

Invitation

Radiant Web

1. Fold white construction paper in half.
2. On the front, draw a web and write "RADIANT" on it using glow-in-the-dark or invisible ink.
3. Write the party details inside using the same ink.
4. Use regular ink to address the envelope. Write instructions for viewing the invitation on the back of the envelope. (If you use invisible ink, make sure to enclose a decoder marker.)

Costumes

Suggest that guests come dressed as characters from the book. Or ask your guests to come dressed for a county fair. Provide accessories when they arrive, such as hats, bandannas, and so on. Or tell your guests to come dressed as funny fair performers, such as a two-headed person, completely hairy person, or three-eyed person.

Decorations

- Paint large boxes to use as game booths. Write the name of a game on the front of each box. Make ticket and snack booths, too.
- Paint a box green and write "Zuckerman's Famous Pig" on it in gold letters.

- Decorate with colorful balloons, streamers, and typical signs found at the fairs, such as "Animal Judging," "Pie-Eating Contest," "Cotton Candy," and "Fun House." Add a few fun signs, such as "Do NOT Enter—Ferocious Animals Inside!" and "House of Horror—Do You Dare?"
- Play band music, such as marches by John Philip Sousa.
- Tape pictures of farm animals to the walls.

- Set out stuffed animals.
- Cover the table with a colorful tablecloth. Make balloon place mats from colored construction paper.

Games

Ring Toss

At a game booth, set soda bottles each a hand's width apart on a card table or TV tray. Give the first player five rings cut from cardboard. Make sure the rings are large enough to fit

around the bottle necks. Have the player stand a few feet away from the table and try to toss all the rings onto the bottles to win a prize.

Pick a Prize

Place several small prizes in a large box. Give the first player two long dowels. Tell her she can pick any prize she wants, but she must pick it up using the two sticks! If she drops the prize

Prizes and Favors
- *Charlotte's Web* by E. B. White
- Toy pigs
- Plastic spiders
- Rubber rats
- Cotton candy

before she gets it out of the box, she loses her turn. Let each player have a turn until he gets a prize.

Word Search

Make a list of words associated with the book, such as "pig," "spider," "rat," "humble," "radiant," "web," and so on. Give each player a magazine, scissors, paper, and glue. Have the kids look through their magazines to find all the words on the list. When they find the words, they should cut them out and glue them onto the paper. The first player to find all the words wins a prize. Or set a time limit for the search and award the prize to the player with the most words when time runs out.

Activities

Web Weaver

Give each guest a circle of plastic craft grid, beads, and multicolored yarn. Have the kids weave yarn patterns to make their circles look like webs. Have them weave words, such as "SOME PIG," "TERRIFIC," "RADIANT," or "HUMBLE." When the webs are finished, hold a web exhibit. Have the guests vote for the most creative web, the most colorful web, and so on.

Animal Faces

Set face paints and several mirrors on the table. Let the kids paint one another's faces to look like the faces of Wilbur, Charlotte, Templeton, and so on. If you have an instant camera, take photos of the "animals" for the kids to take home.

Refreshments

- Homemade fudge
- Individual fruit pies
- Corn dogs
- Cracker Jack, peanuts, and popcorn
- Candied apples
- Raspberry soda

Harriet the Spy

I spy a party! Sneak on over with Harriet the Spy and investigate the fun. You're bound to stumble upon all kinds of things!

Invitation

Invisible Code

1. Write the party details on fancy paper using invisible ink.
2. On the front, explain in small letters how your guest can learn the party details by coloring over the invitation with the decoder marker.
3. Make sure you enclose a decoder marker.

Costumes

Ask your guests to come dressed as Harriet or as their favorite detectives or spies. Provide spy belts with small flashlights, note pads, pens, and water canteens when guests arrive.

Decorations

- Hang plastic magnifying glasses from the ceiling.
- In a corner of the room, set up a tent for secret meetings.
- Tape down footprint cutouts that lead up the walk and inside to the party room.
- Ask the guests to make up their own secret codes and special knocks to use when they arrive at the front door.
- Decorate the room all in yellow like Ole Golly's room.

Games

Observation and Detection

Gather the guests in a circle and give them one minute to silently observe

one another. Then choose a player to leave the room and have her change one thing about her appearance. For example, she could remove her watch, take down her ponytail, or take off her shoes. When she returns to the room, the rest must figure out what's different about her. The first person to guess the change wins a prize and gets to be the next player to leave the room.

Eyewitness

Gather the kids in a room and offer them a snack. Turn on a video camera and aim it toward the center of the room. As the kids are busy eating, have an adult suddenly enter the room, cause a scene, grab something, say something, and leave. Turn off the video camera. Give paper and pencil to each eyewitness. Have the kids write down everything they saw and heard as if they were reporting the commotion to the police. Play the videotape and see how accurate they were with their reports. Award a prize to the most accurate eyewitness.

Hide-and-Seek the Clues

Hide a treasure chest filled with prizes somewhere in the house or yard. Write a set of clues in riddle form, such as "Watching TV is so much fun. By the TV you'll find Clue 1." Write each clue so it leads to the next clue and eventually to the treasure. Divide the players into teams and give each team a different set of clues. At the word "Go!" have them follow their clues until one team reaches the treasure.

Prizes and Favors

- *Harriet the Spy* by Louise Fitzhugh
- Magnifying glasses
- Disposable "spy" cameras

Activities

Spy Newsletter

Hand out paper, pencils, and markers and let the kids write whatever they want: a cartoon, poem, gossip column, advertisement, and so on. When everyone is finished, trim then glue the masterpieces to fit onto a large sheet of paper to make a newsletter. While the party continues, have someone run to the copy store and make a copy of the newsletter for each guest to take home.

Fingerprints

Give each guest a strip of poster board. Have the kids write their names on their strips. Roll each guest's thumb and fingers on an ink pad and then roll her prints onto her strip. Then have each guest make one fingerprint on an index card. Have the kids clean their hands with baby wipes. Mix up the index cards and give one to each guest. Set out the strips of full prints and have the guests match the single prints to the full prints.

Refreshments

- Tomato sandwiches with mayonnaise
- Chocolate Creams: Blend 1 cup club soda, 1 cup milk, and 1 tablespoon chocolate syrup until frothy. Makes 2 servings.
- Spy Cake: Decorate a frosted cake with spy tools such as a magnifying glass, dark sunglasses, and a flashlight.

Harry Potter and the Sorcerer's Stone

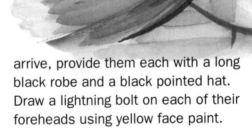

Turn the Muggles into sorcerers at your *Harry Potter* party and you'll have a magical time. Teach a few spells, whip up some potions, and watch the fun appear right before your eyes. It's time for a visit to Hogwarts School of Witchcraft and Wizardry—but watch out for You-Know-Who!

Invitation

Wizard Scroll

1. Write the party details on silver paper using gold or black ink.
2. Burn the edges of the paper to make it look old.
3. Roll up the paper and tie it with silver ribbon.
4. Enclose 3 gold Galleons (gold coin candy).
5. Sprinkle a little glitter in the envelope.

Costumes

Tell the guests to come dressed as Harry or as other characters from the book. Or suggest that guests come dressed as witches and wizards of their own creations. Or when they arrive, provide them each with a long black robe and a black pointed hat. Draw a lightning bolt on each of their foreheads using yellow face paint.

Decorations

- Draw a map of Harry's world, including the Dursley home, King's Cross where Harry catches the Hogwarts Express, Hagrid's hut, and so on. Tape the map to the wall.
- Put up signs marking various locales, including the Leaky Cauldron pub, Diagon Alley, the Apothecary, and so on. Don't forget to include signs for

the four Hogwarts houses: Gryffindor, Hufflepuff, Ravenclaw and Slytherin.

• Set out items from the book, such as an owl, broom, cape, wand, cauldron, telescope, stuffed cat, rubber toad, and so on.

• Make book covers with the following titles and stack them around the room: *The Standard Book of Spells (Grade 1), A History of Magic, One Thousand Magical Herbs and Fungi, Magical Drafts and Potions,* and *Fantastic Beasts and Where to Find Them.*

• Create ghosts like Nearly Headless Nick and Peeves from white construction paper or fabric and hang them from the ceiling.

• Fill a tiny cauldron (or bowl) with gold Galleons and use it as a centerpiece.

Games

Not Quite Quidditch

Use a soccer ball as a Quaffle. Prop up three Hula Hoops at each end of the yard. Divide the players into two teams and give each player a broom or a stick to "ride." The teams must

kick the Quaffle through a hoop. The "keepers" must try to keep the Quaffle from going through their teams' hoops. A team gets ten points each time it kicks the Quaffle through the other team's hoop. Play for a set amount of time and award a prize to the team with the most points when time is up.

Wizard's Thinking Hat

Make a wizard's hat by rolling poster board into a cone shape. Tape the edges to make a hat. Have one player wear the thinking hat and sit on a stool in the middle of the room. Ask her a question about the Harry Potter stories, such as "What are the names of the members of the Dursley family?" "Who is Voldemort?" "Where did Harry live at the Dursley house?" "How old was Harry when he first went to Hogwarts?" and so on. If she can

Prizes and Favors
- *Harry Potter and the Sorcerer's Stone* or other books in the series by J. K. Rowling
- Chess sets
- Magic tricks
- Rubber rats

answer the question, she gets a point and can try to answer another question. If she misses, she must leave the stool and give the hat to another player. The player with the most points wins a prize.

Activities

Mirror Messages

Give each guest pencil, paper, and a mirror. Have them each write a secret message to another guest. However, they must write the messages backward! When all the messages are written, have the guests exchange messages and then read them with their mirrors.

Professor Flitwick's Magic Potion

Collect ingredients for making cookies, pudding, or another treat. Don't tell the kids what you're planning to make. Write the recipe as if it were for a magical potion, renaming the ingredients for fun. For example, you might call flour "cloud dust," milk "ghost's blood," and an egg "dragon snot." Hide the ingredients in containers. Have the kids make the potion following the magical recipe.

Refreshments

- Bertie Bott's Every Flavor Beans (jellybeans)
- Drooble's Best Blowing Gum (bubble gum)
- Chocolate Frogs (Turtle chocolates)
- Pumpkin Pasties (individual pumpkin pies)
- Cauldron Cakes (cupcakes)
- Licorice Wands (licorice)

How to Eat Fried Worms

Billy bets he can eat a worm a day for fifteen days in order to win money for a new minibike. Luckily, Billy is creative and he covers the taste of the worms in everything from ketchup to honey. Do you think you could eat a worm? Have a *How to Eat Fried Worms* party and find out!

Invitation

Gummi Worm to Go

1. Draw a picture of a worm on construction paper.
2. Above the picture, write "You're invited to a How to Eat Fried Worms party. Have you got the nerve?" Below it, write the party details.
3. Punch a hole in the worm's head and poke a Gummi worm through the hole.

Costumes

Ask the kids to come dressed as characters from the book. The characters mostly wore T-shirts and shorts, so when they arrive, you might give them nametags that read "Billy," "Alan," "Tom," "Joe," and so on. Have the guests call one another by these names throughout the party. Or challenge your guests to creatively accessorize their costumes with rubber worms.

Decorations

- In the back yard or garage, set up crates for tables and milking stools for chairs. Or use old wooden boxes, picnic benches, mismatched chairs, and so on.
- Set yellow paper plates on the table and place a big silver platter filled with Gummi worms in the center.

- Hang Gummi worms on fishing line from the ceiling.
- Sprinkle rubber worms on the ground.
- Make worm menus and set one at each place setting. Include choices like "Fried Worms with Ketchup," "Boiled Worms in Cheese Sauce," "Stewed Worms and Horseradish," "Frozen Worms with Cherries on Top," and so on. Don't forget worm drinks like "Wormy Milkshake," "Diet Worm Soda," and "Hot Worm Milk."

Games

Worm Dip Taste Test

Into separate bowls, pour a small amount of the condiments Billy uses to cover the worm taste: ketchup, Worcestershire sauce, mustard, piccalilli, lemon juice, cheese sauce, cherry juice, horseradish, and honey. Add a few more flavors if you like, such as pizza sauce, peanut butter, jelly, melted butter, and spaghetti sauce. Blindfold each player and have him dip a Gummi worm into a condiment and taste it. The player must

correctly identify the condiment to win a prize. Have each player taste a different condiment.

Worm Obstacle Course

Divide the players into two teams and give each team a bike. Sprinkle rubber worms on the ground to make an

Prizes and Favors
- *How to Eat Fried Worms* by Thomas Rockwell
- Rubber or plastic worms
- Worm farms
- Bike accessories
- Piggy banks

obstacle course. Have each teammate take a turn weaving his bike around the worms. If a player rides over a worm, he must return to the starting line. For an added challenge, have each player ride through the obstacle course while balancing a rubber worm on his head. If the worm falls off, he must return to the starting line. Award a prize to the first team to successfully ride through the obstacle course.

Feel a Wiggler

Place several Gummi worms and one real worm in a paper bag. Seat the players in a circle and pass the bag around. Give each player one chance to reach in the bag and try to retrieve the real worm. The player gets a prize if he finds it. Put the worm back in the bag and have the next player try to find it. When the game is over, return the worm to the earth.

Activities

Edible Worms

Set out bowls of bean paste, cookie dough, peanut butter, mashed potatoes, and so on. Have each player select a bowl and make a worm out of the contents. For added fun, blindfold one player and have him taste the different worms and guess what they're made of.

The Worms Crawl In

Sing "The Worms Crawl In": "The worms crawl in, the worms crawl out, the worms crawl over your skull and snout." Have the kids make up new verses.

Refreshments

- Deep-fried worms (fish sticks)
- Peanut-butter-and-Gummi-worm sandwiches
- Whizbang Worm Delights: Ice cream topped with syrup, whipped cream, and Gummi worms
- Worm Froth: Blend a banana and milk. Serve with a Gummi worm hanging over the side of the glass.

Island of the Blue Dolphins

What would it be like to spend time on a faraway island? Be a castaway at an *Island of the Blue Dolphins* party and find out if you can survive the fun!

Invitation

Blue Dolphin

1. Draw the outline of a dolphin on blue plastic.
2. Cut out the dolphin and add eyes and other details with permanent marker.
3. Write party details on a plastic baggie using a permanent marker.
4. Place the dolphin inside the baggie and fill it with shredded blue paper.
5. Mail the invitation.

Costumes

Have your guests come dressed in shorts and tops and have them bring their swimsuits and towels, if swimming will be an activity. Give them flip-flops, straw hats, shell necklaces, and plastic flower leis when they arrive. Dot their foreheads with blue face paint to signify that they're unmarried.

Decorations

- If possible, host the party at a swimming pool. Otherwise create a "pool" by covering the party room floor with blue fabric.
- Decorate the area with tiki torches, fishnets, plastic fish, and other beach items.
- Make a canoe out of a large box and paint it brown.
- Scatter bunches of green streamers to create seaweed.
- Set out potted cacti.

- Hang a large construction paper octopus on the fence at the pool or tape it to a wall at home.
- Provide inflated toys and rafts.

Games

Fishing

Find some smooth stones and paint them to look like tropical fish. Drop them into the shallow end of the pool. Let the kids dive into the water to retrieve as many fish as they can. If the party is held at home, hide the fish around the party room. Award a prize to the player who finds the most fish.

Root Taste Test

Thinly slice root plants and vegetables that can be eaten raw, such as carrots, turnips, parsnips, radishes, horseradish, ginger, and so on. Give the players pencils and paper. Have the guests taste each slice and write down what they think they're tasting. The player who identifies the most roots wins a prize.

Net a Bird

Using permanent markers, decorate a tennis ball to look like a bird. Choose one player to be the bird-thrower. Have the bird-thrower stand on one side of the pool (real or fabric). The rest of the players must stand on the opposite side. Each player must jump into the pool (or onto the fabric pool) as the bird-thrower tosses the bird to him. If a player catches the bird before she hits the water, she gets a point. Award a prize to the player with the most points.

Activities

Castaways

On a table, set out items, such as paper, string, hair clip, sock, towel, pen, paper bag, plastic knife, piece of wood, sponge, hat, and so on. Have each guest choose an item. Tell the castaways they have two minutes to think up a creative and useful way to use their selected items on an island. Have them share their ideas with one another.

Prizes and Favors

- *Island of the Blue Dolphins* by Scott O'Dell
- Shells
- Toy dolphins
- Toy birds
- Books on gardening, animals, and birds

Grass Skirts

Give the kids each a one-inch-wide strip of elastic cut to fit around the waist. Have them staple green streamers to the elastic. Wrap the skirts around the guests' waists and staple them closed. Have the kids dance the hula.

Seashell Scenes

Give each guest stiff white paper and a variety of seashells. Let them create collages using the shells and craft supplies, such as glue, glitter, jewels, markers, paint, and so on.

Refreshments

- Shellfish, clams, oysters, and abalone
- Fish sticks or fillets
- Tuna sandwiches
- Carrot salad
- Red apples

The Lion, the Witch and the Wardrobe

With a little imagination, you can turn your party room into the wondrous wardrobe where you magically pass into the world of Narnia. But watch out for the White Queen—she may keep you in the wardrobe world forever!

Invitation

Wondrous Wardrobe

1. Fold the sides of white construction paper to meet in the middle to make the wardrobe doors.
2. Round the top corners of the card with scissors. Draw then cut out a centered, narrow rectangle from the bottom of the card, leaving enough card on both sides of the rectangle for the wardrobe "legs." Draw door handles.
3. On the doors, write "Welcome to the Wardrobe."
4. Open the doors and write the party details inside.
5. Use "Narnia" as a return address.

Costumes

Ask the guests to come dressed as characters from the book, such as Peter, Susan, Edmund, Lucy, a faun, a centaur, Aslan, Father Christmas, or the White Queen. Or suggest that guests come dressed completely in white for Narnia, the land of constant winter.

Decorations

• Welcome the guests by having them crawl through a "wardrobe" made from a large box. Drape coats over the wardrobe so the guests have to push through them. On the other

side of the wardrobe, spread out "snow" made from a white sheet or cotton batting covering the floor, furniture, and table.

- Hang paper snowflakes from the ceiling.
- Hang icicle lights.
- Put up a sign that reads "Welcome to Narnia."
- In another room, make a springlike atmosphere complete with flowers, grass (made from green fabric), pictures of birds, and so on.

- Put out stuffed animals that represent the animals in the book.
- Use a small stone statue as a centerpiece.
- Display the gifts the siblings received from Father Christmas: a bow and arrow, horn, sword with a gold handle, shield featuring a red lion, glass bottle filled with a red liquid that can cure anything, and small dagger.
- Cover a chair with velvet to make a throne and hang a sign that reads "Cair Paravel" above it.

Games

Coat Race

Divide the players into two teams. Give each team a coat and have the first players put them on but not fasten them closed. Have the players join hands with the next teammates in line. The players must pass the coats to their teammates by twisting and wiggling but not by letting go of hands. The first team to have all of its teammates wear the coat wins a prize.

Frozen Statues

Have a player freeze like a statue, pretending to be a character from the book, such as a centaur, unicorn, lion, wolf, satyr, and so on. The next player must try to identify the character. If she guesses correctly, both players get a point, and the guessing player freezes into the next statue. If she guesses incorrectly, the next player gets to guess. Let everyone have a turn freezing into a statue. Award a prize to the player with the most points.

Prizes and Favors

- *The Lion, the Witch and the Wardrobe* or other books in the series by C. S. Lewis
- Toy lions
- Toy horns, bows and arrows, swords and shields, and daggers
- Decorative containers filled with Turkish delight or taffy

Activities

Swords and Shields

Cut cardboard swords (round the tips for safety) and shields for each guest. Let the kids paint the blades silver and the hilts gold and black. Have them paint lions or other creatures on the shields. Provide decorative jewels to glue onto the shields.

King or Queen for a Day

Choose one guest to dress up as a king or queen. Give him or her a cardboard sword and seat him or her on the Cair Paravel throne. Have each guest come up to the king or queen and be knighted or be made a lady. The king or queen should give the knights and ladies new names and present them with their newly decorated swords.

Turkish Delight and Tea

Set up a tea party in the spring room. Seat the guests at small tables set with teacups and plates. Serve them Turkish delight (or any kind of taffy) along with fruity herbal tea. Offer ham sandwiches or toast on the side.

Refreshments

- Fish and chips
- Hard-boiled eggs
- Toast with butter, honey, sardines, or tuna
- Frosted cake topped with colored sprinkles
- Snowballs: Shape a scoop of ice cream into a ball. Roll the ice cream ball in coconut. Refreeze before serving.

Little Women

The four March girls invite you to their party that calls for dressing up, drama, drawing, and dining. Join in the fun as Beth, Meg, Amy, and Jo entertain you and your friends in true American style.

Invitation

March Paper Dolls

1. Draw 5 female paper dolls on white paper.
2. Label 4 of the paper dolls "Amy," "Beth," "Meg," and "Jo" and label the middle paper doll with the guest's name.
3. Write party details around the dolls.

Costumes

Encourage guests to come in ankle-length dresses. Provide costume accessories, such as old-fashioned gloves, bonnets, or button-up boots, when they arrive. Or have guests come dressed as one of the March sisters or as other characters from the book, such as Laurie or Mr. Lawrence.

Decorations

- Set up a theater for the March girls' plays: Hang sheets or crepe paper for curtains, lay plywood for the stage, and shine extra lights on the stage.
- Play piano or harpsichord music.
- Set out drawing paper and art supplies.
- Set out a box of costumes and accessories.
- Decorate with embroidered pillows, sheet music, vases of paper flowers, and lots and lots of books.

• Set a Victorian table with teacups and a teapot, a plate of petit fours, fresh flowers, and a copy of *Little Women.*

Games

Tell the Truth

On index cards, have the players write questions their friends must answer truthfully. Place the cards facedown in a bowl labeled "Truth." On another set of index cards, have the players write stunts their friends must perform if they choose not to answer questions. Place the cards facedown in a bowl labeled "Dare." Have a player draw a card from the Truth bowl and read it out loud. The player now has a choice: Answer the question truthfully or draw a stunt card from the Dare bowl. Award prizes to those who tell the truth and to those who perform dares.

Crazy Croquet

Set up a croquet obstacle course, using chairs, coffee tables, stools, and so on for wickets. Give the first player a rubber ball and a mallet and time how long it takes her to complete the course. Repeat for each player. Award a prize to the player with the fastest time.

Activities

Art Tables

Place different art supplies on separate tables. For example, set one table with drawing pads and charcoal, another with tissue paper and wire, another with watercolors and water-color paper, and another with paper, paints, and paintbrushes. Divide the players into small groups. Rotate the groups so each visits every art supply table and every player can create a work of art with the supplies.

Put on a Play!

Let the guests write their own play or borrow a short play from the library. Provide lots of costumes and accessories. Let the kids decorate the set using cardboard, paint, and fabric. Provide interesting props to stimulate imagination, such as a mystery box, butterfly net, walking stick, towel, pizza cutter, stuffed animal, deck of cards, and so on. Videotape the play and show it to the guests at the end of the party.

Prizes and Favors

- *Little Women* or *Little Men* by Louisa May Alcott
- Art supplies, such as markers, watercolors, colored chalk, and drawing pads
- Embroidery starter kits
- Journals
- Pens or quills

Rigamarole

The first guest begins a story and continues telling it for one minute. After a minute, she must stop, and the next guest must pick up where the story left off. Continue until everyone has had a turn adding to the story. The last guest must finish the story. Play again, each time picking a new genre, such as romance, mystery, science fiction, and so on.

Refreshments

- Strawberry and vanilla ice cream
- Cake frosted pink and white
- Fruit
- Chocolate or ice cream bonbons
- Decaffeinated mochas in mugs
- Serve lunch under a tent like the March girls did at the boating party.
- Serve sandwiches from picnic baskets.

Mrs. Frisby and the Rats of NIMH

What do you do when you find out rats are smarter than humans? Have a party and celebrate! Join Mrs. Frisby, her children, and all the other brilliant rats of NIMH as they try to save their home and their secret lives.

Invitation

Mrs. Frisby's Cheese

1. Fold yellow construction paper in half.
2. Glue a picture of Mrs. Frisby inside.
3. Cut a small hole in the front so Mrs. Frisby's face peeks out.
4. Draw black circles on the front to make "holes" in the "cheese."
5. Write the party details inside.
6. Glue a piece of gray or white yarn on the back so it looks as if Mrs. Frisby's tail is hanging out.
7. Mail in a yellow envelope covered with black dots to look like Swiss cheese.

Costumes

Have the kids come dressed as rats. Or turn the guests into rats when they arrive. Make ears by attaching stiff black felt or black craft foam onto headbands. Draw on eyebrow-pencil whiskers. Make rat noses from cone-shaped party hats. Pin rope tails to pants. Give the kids nametags each labeled with a character's name, such as Mrs. Frisby, Teresa, Martin, Cynthia, Timothy, Jeremy, Mr. Ages, Jonathan, Nicodemus, Justin, Brutus, Arthur, and so on.

Decorations

- Welcome the guests with a big banner that reads "Thorn Valley."

- Put up signs that read "Frisby Farm," "Owl's Tree," "The Laboratory," "Fitzgibbon's Farm," and "Beware of Cat!"
- Create a farmhouse for the Frisbys from a large box.
- Create a laboratory by covering a table with bowls and glasses for experiments.
- Set out stuffed mice and rats and tape pictures of mice and rats to the walls.
- Paint small boxes to look like Swiss cheese and use them as decorations and as a centerpiece.

- Blow up balloons and draw rat faces on them with permanent marker. Tie on ribbons for tails.

Games

Shocking Shapes

The rats had to match shapes to avoid receiving electric shocks. We won't go that far, but here's a game that matches wits with the rats. Before the game, cut several lightning bolts from yellow construction paper. Give the players pencils and paper. At the word "Go!" the players have one minute to write down all the circles they see in the party room, such as a round coffee table, coaster, fishbowl, and so on. The player who writes down the most circles wins a prize. The winner then gets to "shock" the other players by taping lightning bolts to their shirts. Play again using squares, triangles, rectangles, or other shapes. The player with the most lightning bolts wins a booby prize.

Grain Race

Fill two plastic buckets with rice, sand, birdseed, or another grainy substance. Divide the players into two teams and give each team a large container. Set the buckets of grain at one end of the yard and the containers at the other end. At the word "Go!" the first players must scoop the grain with large spoons, race to the other side, dump the grain into their containers, return to their teams, and hand the spoons to the next teammates in line, who must repeat the tasks. Play for three minutes, then stop the race. Measure

the amount of grain in each team's container. Award a prize to the team that transported the most grain into its container.

Rat Race Maze

Divide the players into two teams. Give each team about thirty to fifty feet of rope. Send one team into the front yard and the other into the back yard. Have them wind the rope around the yard to make a maze for the other team. Time the teams as they race through the mazes one player at a time. The fastest team to run through its maze wins a prize.

Activities

Rat Residence

Divide the kids into small groups and assign each group a large box. Give them paint, markers, pictures, fabric, glue, scissors, decals, stickers, carpet squares, and other decorating supplies. Let the kids turn the boxes into rat cottages. When the cottages are finished, let the groups visit one another's cottages, hide inside them, and so on. Let them eat their snacks inside their cottages, too.

Miniature Rat Houses

Ask the kids each to bring a shoebox to the party. Or provide them yourself. Provide craft supplies, such as markers, fabric, glitter, ribbon, stickers,

Prizes and Favors

- *Mrs. Frisby and the Rats of NIMH* by Robert C. O'Brien
- Toy mice or rats
- Individually wrapped miniature cheeses
- Chemistry kits
- Maze books

decals, glue, and scissors, to turn the shoeboxes into miniature rat homes. Provide miniature furniture to add to the houses, such as chairs, tables, beds, and so on. Or have the kids make their own furniture using construction paper and poster board. Give them rat figurines to live in the finished houses.

NIMH Laboratory Experiments

Pour 1 cup cornstarch into a plastic baggie for each guest. Let the kids slowly add ¼ cup water mixed with a few drops of food coloring to their baggies. (Add more water a few drops at a time if mixture is too dry.) Carefully press excess air from the baggies and seal them with duct tape. Knead the bags until the mixture is smooth. Let the kids handle their mixtures. The mixture should change from soft to firm as it's being manipulated.

Refreshments

- A variety of cereals for the kids to make their own bowls of grains
- Small or cut-up fruit to add to the cereals, such as berries, bananas, and raisins
- Corn on the cob and other farm vegetables
- Cheese
- Swiss Cheese Cake: Frost a round cake yellow and dot it with round chocolate mints to make "holes" in the "cheese."

The Secret Garden

Come join us in the secret garden where Mary Lennox learned how to plant seeds, remove weeds, and enjoy animals, and where sickly Colin bloomed along with the flowers. We'll have a garden party of our own!

Invitation

Flower Seed Packet

1. Carefully slit open a packet of flower seeds.
2. Write party details on a slip of paper and insert it into the seed packet.
3. Seal the packet with tape.
4. Write "Open Me!" on it with marker.
5. Place the seed packet in the envelope along with dried flowers or leaves.

Costumes

Ask guests to come dressed as characters from the book, such as Mary, Archibald, Colin, Dickon, Ben, and so on. The guests could also come dressed as animals from the book, such as Soot the crow, Jump the pony, Captain the fox, or the squirrels Nut and Shell. Or suggest that the guests come dressed as gardeners. Offer the guests costume accessories when they arrive, such as gardening gloves, gardening aprons, straw hats, and so on.

Decorations

- Host the party in the back yard or at a park. Or create your own "garden" in the party room by taping pictures of flowers and plants to the walls.
- Make a secret doorway with crepe paper or bed sheets for the kids to crawl through to get to the "garden."

- Use a bowl of flowers as a centerpiece. Or use an artificial bird nest as a centerpiece and prop up gardening tools against it.
- On a packet of seeds, cover the name of the seed with correcting fluid and replace it with a guest's name. Photocopy different packets of seeds, enlarge the copies, and use them as place mats.
- Hang streamers from the ceiling to create garden vines.
- Tape trees made from construction paper to the walls.

Games

Fruit or Vegetable?

Collect a number of fruits and vegetables—some easy to identify and some more difficult, such as kiwi fruit, eggplant, kumquat, and squash. Be sure you know which ones are fruits and which ones are vegetables before you play! Give the players paper and pencils. Have them classify each item as either a fruit or a vegetable. The player who correctly classifies the most items wins a prize. For added fun, give the players a taste of the fruits and vegetables after the game.

Flower Hunt

Hide a variety of real or fake flowers all over the house or yard. Teach the players how to identify the various flowers you've hidden. Give them pencils and paper to take notes if they'd like. Divide the players into teams and give each team a list of flowers to find. The first team to return with all the flowers on its list wins a prize.

Prizes and Favors
- *The Secret Garden* by Frances Hodgson Burnett
- Packets of seeds
- Flowers in small vases
- Jump ropes

Gardening Glove Touch-and-Tell

Put items related to the book in separate paper bags, such as a jump rope, packet of seeds, stuffed animal, vegetable, garden glove, trowel, flower, and so on. Have the players wear gardening gloves and give them paper and pencils. Have the players reach inside each bag and feel the item without looking. They must write down their guesses about what's in the bag while still wearing gardening gloves. After everyone has felt inside each bag, reveal the items to the players. The player who correctly identifies the most items wins a prize.

Jump Rope Contests

Give the kids jump ropes and let them have jump rope contests. Who can jump the longest with her eyes closed, on one leg, or backward? Who can jump the fastest? Let the players make up their own contests as well. Award a prize to the winner of each contest.

Activities

Herb Gardens

Give each guest a small jar and some herb seeds. Let the kids fill their jars with potting soil and then plant their seeds. Have them take the herbs home to watch them grow.

Nature Walk

Give the kids a list of items to find along a nature walk in the park, such as a blue flower, thorn, dead leaf, pine needle, acorn, weed, bush, fruit tree, and so on. Have them check off each item they find. Encourage them to note any other interesting items they come across. Have the kids compare lists when the walk is over.

Gardening Glove Puppets

Give each guest one plain gardening glove. Set out pompoms, markers, googly eyes, felt scraps, pipe cleaners, and other decorating supplies along with scissors and glue. Have the kids make puppets out of their gloves.

Refreshments

- Veggies and dips
- Stuffed potatoes
- Individual fruit pies
- Currant buns, crumpets, and muffins with jam and clotted cream
- Fruit drinks
- Edible nuts and seeds
- Edible flowers from a flower shop or gourmet grocery store

Treasure Island

Nothing brings pirates to life like Robert Louis Stevenson's classic adventure book. You can bring the pirate party to life with mysterious maps, treasure hunts, Jolly Rogers, and pieces of eight! Join us, ye swab, for we're settin' sail to Treasure Island!

Invitation

Mystery Map

1. Fray the edges of yellow construction paper and color them brown so they look centuries old.
2. Using markers, label each guest's home and the party home on the map.
3. Add Treasure Island landmarks, such as Spyglass Hill, Skeleton Island, Mizzenmast Hill, as well as swamps, graves, and stockades. Be sure to draw a compass on the map.
4. Write party details on the back.
5. Roll the map and tie it with ribbon.
6. Paint a paper towel tube gold to look like a telescope.
7. Insert the scroll into the telescope and mail or hand-deliver it to your guest in a cardboard tube.

Costumes

Invite your guests to come dressed as pirates or provide them with bandannas, gold earrings, pirate hats, big-buckle belts, and so on when they arrive. You might even want to safety-pin stuffed parrots to their shoulders. Ask the guests to name themselves after the pirates from the book, such as Billy Bones, Flint, Long John Silver, Black Dog, or Smollett. Or have them think up their own pirate names.

Decorations

- Welcome the guests with a big black spot cutout taped to the door. Place black spot cutouts around the party room, too, and use them as place mats.
- Cover the table with a gold or black tablecloth. Sprinkle costume jewelry, play money, and chocolate gold coins on the tablecloth.
- For a centerpiece, paint a small box to look like a treasure chest and place a stuffed parrot on top to guard the treasure.
- Create Treasure Island by laying brown or green fabric on the floor. Tape a construction paper tree to a nearby wall.
- Make a pirate ship out of a large box. Hoist the Jolly Roger flag and set the ship in the middle of the room. Name it the *Hispaniola.*
- Hang Jolly Roger and Union Jack flags from the ceiling.
- Play pirate music, such as *Bedtime Stories for Pirates* by Captain Bogg & Salty.

Games

Pieces of Eight Hunt

Hide a treasure somewhere in the house. Two teams will hunt for this treasure. For the first team, choose five locations in the house. Starting from the front door, write directions to one location, such as "16 paces forward, 2 paces right, 10 paces forward." Place a gold chocolate coin, or "piece of eight," at this first location along with a set of directions to the second location. At the second location, leave another piece of eight and a set of directions to the third location, and so on. At the fifth location, leave a piece of eight and directions to the treasure. Repeat this process for the second team, but choose five new locations for their pieces of eight. At game time, divide the players into two teams. Start each team at the front door and give them their first sets of directions. At the word "Go!" have them follow their directions to the first piece of eight, and so on. The first

team to collect all five pieces of eight and find the treasure wins the booty.

Walk the Plank

Set several two-by-fours around the back yard to make a winding "plank." Have the pirates walk the plank one at a time, assigning them a different stunt to do each time. For example, have a player walk heel-to-toe, sideways, backward, turning around as she goes, or with her arms at her sides. Each time a pirate makes it across without stepping off the plank, award him a point. The player with the most points wins a prize. The rest, unfortunately, have been eaten by crocodiles.

Activities

Swords

Cut swords from cardboard or poster board. Round the tips for safety. Let the kids decorate their swords with gold, silver, and black paint as well as with markers, glitter, and stickers.

Raise the Jolly Roger

Give each guest a square of white fabric. Let the guests design and create their own pirate flags with their squares using markers, fabric paints, and decals. Attach each flag to a long stick and have the guests name their flags.

Prizes and Favors

- *Treasure Island* by Robert Louis Stevenson
- Telescopes and compasses
- Jolly Roger flags
- Chocolate gold coins and costume jewelry

Eye Patches

Have guests make their own eye patches using small circles of black, plastic-coated fabric or leatherette. Using a turkey skewer or leather-sewing needle, punch holes for the kids on each side of their patches. Have each guest tie the ends of black string or elastic string (long enough to fit around his head) to the holes. Have the guests put on their eye patches and play some games that require hand-eye coordination, such as catch.

Refreshments

- Treasure Chest Cake: Frost a sheet cake brown and cover it with candy jewels and chocolate gold coins.
- Grog (fruit punch served in big mugs)
- Sandwiches cut in the shape of pirate hats
- Cheese, apples, raisins, and bis-cuits
- Yo-Ho-Hos (Ho Hos snack cakes)

The Wind in the Willows

Join Mole, Ratty, Toad, Otter, and Badger on a wacky water adventure and picnic party! Hold onto your seats—it's going to be a wild ride!

Invitation

Mole's Hole

1. Draw or photocopy a picture of Mole.
2. Fold brown construction paper in half.
3. Cut a circle from the front.
4. Glue Mole inside, but do not glue down his head.
5. Write the party details below Mole.
6. Stick Mole's head through the hole and close the card.
7. Enclose a few blades of grass.

Costumes

Invite guests to come dressed as characters from the story. When they arrive, use face paint to make their faces look like the characters' faces. Give them animal ears made out of stiff felt or craft foam attached to headbands and tails made of fake fur or rope.

Decorations

- Set up a picnic area outside with a large blanket and picnic basket.
- Float small boats in a wading pool.
- Make signs for the characters and set them around the yard where they might live, such as Mole's Hole, Ratty's Hole, Badger's Hole, Otter's Pool, and Toad Hall.
- Make signs for popular spots in the book, such as the river, the picnic area, the boat races, the country, and so on.
- Set stuffed animals all over the yard.

Games

Ratty's Boat Races

Give each player a small plastic boat. Let them write names on the boats using permanent markers. Have two players place their boats on one side of the wading pool. At the word "Go!" have them splash their boats to the other side. The player whose boat first reaches the other side must race the next player's boat. Continue the race until everyone has had a turn racing a boat. Award a prize to the grand champion.

Cloud Contest

Have the players lie down on the picnic blanket and look up at the sky. Ask them to watch the clouds. Hand out white paper, pencils, and scissors. Have each player cut the paper into a cloud shape. Pass around one cloud and have each guest write on a separate piece of paper what shape he thinks it is. After everyone has seen the cloud, ask the guests what they wrote. Anyone who sees the same shape as another player gets a point. Continue passing around the clouds. The player with the most points wins a prize.

Activities

Picnic Hunt

Make your guests work for their picnic food! Seal the food in separate containers. Hide the containers all over the yard. Have the players search for the containers and bring them back to the picnic table. Don't let anyone eat until all the containers are found.

Prizes and Favors

- *The Wind in the Willows* by Kenneth Grahame
- Toy moles, otters, rats, toads, or badgers
- Toy boats
- Model boats
- Water toys or accessories

Boats

Let the kids create their own boats out of balsa wood, margarine tubs, wood scraps, Styrofoam, and other floatable materials. Provide waterproof glue, duct tape, and string. Give the kids paint, permanent markers, stickers, and decals to decorate their finished boats. Take the boats to the wading pool and see if they float!

Picnic Baskets

Give each guest a small wicker basket along with paints, markers, ribbon, and other craft supplies to decorate their baskets. Fill the baskets with special snacks for the kids to eat at home.

Refreshments

- Ham or roast beef sandwiches on French rolls
- Pickles
- Macaroni or potato salad
- Lemonade or ginger ale
- Ice cream
- Pool Cake: Frost a round cake blue and top it with small plastic boats.

Index

Look for Meadowbrook Press books where you buy books.
You may also order books by using the form printed below.

Order Form

Qty.	Title	Author	Order No.	Unit Cost (U.S. $)	Total
	Bad Case of the Giggles	Lansky, B.	2411	$16.00	
	Craft Fun with Sondra	Clark, S.	3301	$5.95	
	Free Stuff for Kids	Free Stuff Editors	2190	$5.00	
	Fun Family Traditions	MacGregor, C.	2446	$9.00	
	Girls to the Rescue, Book #1	Lansky, B.	2215	$3.95	
	Girls to the Rescue, Book #2	Lansky, B.	2216	$3.95	
	Girls to the Rescue, Book #3	Lansky, B.	2219	$3.95	
	Happy Birthday to Me!	Lansky, B.	2416	$8.95	
	If Pigs Could Fly . . .	Lansky, B.	2431	$15.00	
	Kids' Outdoor Parties	Warner, P.	6045	$8.00	
	Kids' Party Cookbook	Warner, P.	2435	$12.00	
	Kids' Party Games and Activities	Warner, P.	6095	$12.00	
	Kids' Pick-a-Party Book	Warner, P.	6090	$9.00	
	Kids Pick the Funniest Poems	Lansky, B.	2410	$17.00	
	Miles of Smiles	Lansky, B.	2412	$17.00	
	Mommy's Little Helper Cookbook	Brown, K.	2455	$9.00	
	Newfangled Fairy Tales, Book #1	Lansky, B.	2500	$3.95	
	Newfangled Fairy Tales, Book #2	Lansky, B.	2501	$3.95	
	No More Homework! No More Tests!	Lansky, B.	2414	$8.00	
	Poetry Party	Lansky, B.	2430	$15.00	
	Slumber Parties	Warner, P.	6091	$8.00	
	What Do You Know about Manners?	MacGregor, C.	3201	$6.99	
				Subtotal	
			Shipping and Handling (see below)		
			MN residents add 6.5% sales tax		
				Total	

YES! Please send me the books indicated above. Add $2.00 shipping and handling for the first book with a retail price up to $9.99 or $3.00 for the first book with a retail price of over $9.99. Add $1.00 shipping and handling for each additional book. All orders must be prepaid. Most orders are shipped within two days by U.S. Mail (7–9 delivery days). Rush shipping is available for an extra charge. Overseas postage will be billed. **Quantity discounts available upon request.**

Send book(s) to:

Name _____ Address _____

City _____ State _____ Zip _____ Telephone (_____)_____

Payment via:

❑ Check or money order payable to Meadowbrook Press (No cash or COD's please)

❑ Visa (for orders over $10.00 only)   ❑ MasterCard (for orders over $10.00 only)

Account # _____ Signature _____ Exp. Date _____

A *FREE* Meadowbrook Press catalog is available upon request.
You can also phone or fax us with a credit card order.

Mail to: Meadowbrook Press, 5451 Smetana Drive, Minnetonka, MN 55343

Phone 952-930-1100   Toll-Free 800-338-2232   Fax 952-930-1940

For more information (and fun) visit our websites:

www.meadowbrookpress.com   www.gigglepoetry.com